W9-BUW-666

RAGBRAI
Everyone Pronounces It Wrong

RAGBRAI

Everyone Pronounces It Wrong

John Karras and Ann Karras

Iowa State University Press / Ames

ANN KARRAS grew up in New Jersey and met her future husband in college in Pennsylvania. Three children later, the family moved to Des Moines, Iowa. The fourth child is an Iowan. Ann is a medical technologist and a photographer who documented many RAGBRAIs. Her time is now divided between outdoor activities in Iowa and Colorado.

JOHN KARRAS grew up in Cleveland and worked in newspapers from 1952 to 1984 in a variety of mostly editorial jobs. The bike bug bit in 1967. The book describes how a fifteen-mile, three-speed family ride to Camp Dodge somehow evolved into co-founding RAGBRAI.

© 1999 Iowa State University Press
All rights reserved

Iowa State University Press
2121 South State Avenue
Ames, Iowa 50014

Orders: 1-800-862-6657
Office: 1-515-292-0140
Fax: 1-515-292-3348
Web site: www.isupress.edu

RAGBRAI® is a registered trademark of the Des Moines Register and Tribune Company. Used by permission.

RAGBRAI maps reprinted by permission of Dan Caplan, Capp's Sports, Inc., Kansas City, Mo.

Frank Miller cartoon reprinted by permission of M. Catherine Miller.

Brian Duffy cartoon reprinted by permission of Brian Duffy.

Cover photo by Ann Karras.

Book design by Kathy J. Walker.

Authorization to photocopy items for internal or personal use, or the internal or personal use of specific clients, is granted by Iowa State University Press, provided that the base fee of $.10 per copy is paid directly to the Copyright Clearance Center, 222 Rosewood Drive, Danvers, MA 01923. For those organizations that have been granted a photocopy license by CCC, a separate system of payments has been arranged. The fee code for users of the Transactional Reporting Service is 0-8138-2019-7/99 $.10.

♾ Printed on acid-free paper in the United States of America

First edition, 1999

LIBRARY OF CONGRESS CATALOGING-IN-PUBLICATION DATA

Karras, John
   RAGBRAI: everyone pronounces it wrong / John Karras and Ann Karras. —1st edition.
      p. cm.
   Includes bibliographical references (p.) and index.
   ISBN 0-8138-2019-7
   1. RAGBRAI (Bicycle race).
   2. RAGBRAI (Bicycle race)—History.
   3. Bicycle racing—Iowa—History.
   I. Karras, Ann. II. Title.
   GV1049.2.R34K37   1999
   796.6'2'09777—dc21   99-17546

The last digit is the print number:
9 8 7 6 5 4 3 2 1

This book is dedicated to

all the small Iowa towns

that have made

RAGBRAI possible

"Sometimes it's nice just to be a cow."

Contents

Preface A few words are needed about this book.

Ann and I have collaborated on it, both in the research and the writing. It would not have been written without her dedicated and extensive research throughout the writing and, hardly less important, her urging. And, of course, her excellent photographs add immeasurably to the project. The final draft, however, is mine, so that any complaints or disagreements or opprobrium of any kind should be directed at me.

Here is Ann's view of our collaboration:

Most of the art work is mine. My writing, however, has been incorporated anonymously into the body of the work through John's editing. We both spent hours researching, remembering and discussing rides, especially the early years. Our experiences were much the same, but the outlooks often different and our relationship to the ride completely dissimilar.

John worked for *The Register*, mapped the routes, made speeches, met with the Chamber people and wrote stories. I went along in the role of a rider who sometimes filled in as an emergency helper. I would ride by myself or with friends, sometimes with admiring strangers (always wondering what in the world they were admiring), and occasionally behind people engaged in conversation that I could quietly eavesdrop on. Sometimes I would find an individual whom I thought John would like to interview or get an idea he might write about.

I didn't start taking photos until about the fourth ride since *The Register* had its own photographers. As RAGBRAI continued year after year, I became very serious about documenting the rides, but marketing remained a mystery, and I sold very few RAGBRAI photographs. Toward the end of the first twenty-five years, I realized it was more fun just to ride without the weight of cameras, without having to stop for every photo opportunity, without the expense and without the time-consuming task of labeling and researching. But the rides I documented are the most memorable for me.

The book concentrates on the early years—the formative years—of RAGBRAI, when numbers and circumstances changed from year to year at a rate to make one's head spin. I mark the formative years from the first ride in 1973 to the thirteenth in 1985, when all hell broke loose. Along the way and afterward there were many significant changes, which we have attempted to document.

This is not to imply that everything has been hunky-dory since 1985. Far from it. The changes, variations and surprises have continued right up to the present day, but have been more in the nature of fine-tuning than those of the early days. Of course, the end is not in sight at this writing, and it would be both presumptuous and impossible to predict how things eventually will turn out.

In addition to my wife, I must add heartfelt thanks to Lois Peterson, one-time RAGBRAI office manager, who filled huge scrapbooks with voluminous newspaper clippings about all the rides from 1973 through 1985. Without them this book could not have been assembled.

My colleagues and former colleagues (Jim Green, Chuck Offenburger, Don Benson, Lois Peterson) all have been helpful and cooperative. A nod of thanks must go to such dedicated folks as Kay and Ray Reasoner who took on the largely thankless task of driving sag wagons on 18 RAGBRAIs (actually, Kay still drives one; Ray finally figured out in 1996 that cycling RAGBRAI is more fun than sagging it, and has been riding ever since).

There are hundreds, no thousands, more. I would love to thank every one of them by name but time, space and memory fail. The list would fill a large telephone book. I can only thank them by groups:

- The state patrol and the thousands of local police officers, sheriffs' deputies, volunteer firemen and others who directed traffic and helped the thousands of riders through Iowa's many dangerous intersections.
- The many bike shops that have kept RAGBRAI on the road.
- The dedicated and consummately efficient medical folks who've wrapped knees, treated sunburn and road rash for thousands of hurting cyclists.
- The thousands and thousands of Iowans along our thousands of miles of RAGBRAI routes who've fed, watered, applauded, dished up spaghetti and homemade pie in church basements, turned on their hoses to cool us off when the temperature soared, who played music for us, danced with us, entertained us and asked thousands and thousands of questions over the years.
- And finally, there is the staff at the Iowa State University Press. As a long-time former editor (newspapers, not books), I can appreciate a delicate touch with a word or a phrase, and the press's editors could not have been gentler.

Introduction *Everyone Pronounces It Wrong* is an

odd title for a book, don't you think? Let me explain.

I made up the name, *The Register*'s Annual Great Bicycle Ride Across Iowa-III in 1975 (I'll tell you later exactly why). Now you must understand, I meant the acronym to be something of a joke, something that would amuse by virtue of its ponderous length, something that would bring a smile to the lips of anyone speaking it. America was very big on acronyms at the time and has only gotten worse since.

The federal government was the biggest producer of them: Housing and Urban Development (HUD), Strategic Air Command (SAC), Health, Education and Welfare (HEW), North American Air Defense (NORAD), and so it went on endlessly and mindlessly. RAGBRAI was my modest attempt to poke fun at the practice.

And how did the people react? Did they snicker? Did they giggle? Did they applaud my wit? Not on your life. They said, "How do you pronounce that?"

I used to reply, "Any way you want to," and that, of course, is exactly what they did. In short, they all mispronounced it. All except my wife and Kaul and an occasional acquaintance, and even Kaul slips once in a while. Don Benson mispronounces it even though he ran the ride for 19 years. Jim Green, Benson's successor, mispronounces it. Even Iowa Boy Chuck Offenburger, my co-host since 1983, mispronounces it, although he won't admit it.

Worse yet, Green codified the mispronunciation by including ("pronounced RAG-BRYE") in a 1997 press release.

It has been pronounced RAGBREE, RAGABAG, RAGBROW

and, most commonly, RAGBRYE, and I've about had it.

RAGBRAI should be pronounced RAGBRAY, and no other way.

Thus, the title.

(Actually, it isn't my title. Well, it is now, but it really was a gift from a West Des Moines friend, Lou Ann Sandburg. She said at the time, "You should write a book about RAGBRAI before someone else does. You could call it *Everyone Pronounces It Wrong*." I'm still not sure it's a good idea, but here we are).

The diphthong *ai* in American pronunciation rhymes with a long *a*, as in hair, lair, fair, pair, and so on. Only an ignoramus would comb his hire, stare at the giant boar at the state fire, or tell his woman that they make a peach of a pyre (well, maybe once in a while). And yet, some of the best educated, most cultured and most sophisticated people in the nation, if not the world (along with a few klutzes), persist in pronouncing it RAG-BRYE. There's no accounting for some things in this life.

And what is my hope with this broadside? Do I have illusions of repairing the damage, of changing the way folks pronounce the acronym, of changing the course of events? Are you kidding? I'll be 70 years old sooner than I'd like to think. I've seen how things go in this life. I don't expect any of the offenders to change their ways.

At best, at the very best, I hope to feel better for having gotten this off my chest. And a pox on illiterate mispronouncers. No, two poxes, both the small and the large. And if you can't pronounce RAGBRAI correctly you won't have even the faintest idea of what distinguishes the small pox from the large.

Oh, yes, before I forget. The second object of this book, besides trying to shame you into pronouncing RAGBRAI my way (that is to say, the correct way), is to tell you about some of the fun my wife and I and thousands and thousands of others have had through 25 years of this insanity.

A brief overview of what's to come in the pages ahead:

Donald Kaul and I invented RAGBRAI in 1973 without

knowing what we were doing, and operated as co-hosts until 1983; Don Benson of *The Register*'s promotion department ran it for 19 years, through 1991; Jim Green, formerly of *The Register*'s circulation department, apprenticed with Benson in 1991, then took it over in 1992 and has been running it superbly ever since.

Kaul and management got into a disagreement in the spring of 1983 that resulted in Kaul's leaving *The Register*, at which time Chuck Offenburger, author of *The Register*'s Iowa Boy column, joined me as co-host, a friendly relationship that has continued to the present.

Offenburger resigned from *The Register* in June of 1998 but agreed to ride on and write for RAGBRAI-XXVI the next month. Those were his best stories to appear in *The Register*. I'll miss him.

RAGBRAI, the event, started out as little more than an idea that hardly anyone took seriously and in the intervening 25 years has grown into a small industry.

Benson, who wore many hats in his years in the promotion department, never worked on RAGBRAI full-time. Green does, with full-time office help. The first year, we didn't even drive the route. Now we begin planning in December, drive it in February, coordinate it with the state patrol and county engineers and invariably tweak it half a dozen times between February and the last full week of July, when the ride takes place.

The Register charged no RAGBRAI fee until 1983 and sold almost nothing until that same year. In 1997, the fee was $90 per rider, and fees along with sales of a full line of merchandise, including bike jerseys for the first time, grossed a little over a million dollars.

RAGBRAI has come a long way in those years. But remarkably, we have so far been able to maintain the impression, even though everyone knows it isn't true, that it just somehow happens spontaneously. I hope that never changes.

Hope you enjoy it as much as we have.

RAGBRAI
Everyone Pronounces It Wrong

In the Beginning—
the First Ride Donald Kaul and I are going to

ride from Sioux City to Davenport the week of Aug. 26

and we'd like to have as many of you as are able join us along

the way.

That paragraph, appearing in the July 22, 1973, issue of *The Des Moines Register,* was the first I ever wrote about what was to become known as *The Register*'s Annual Great Bicycle Ride Across Iowa. The first of thousands of paragraphs spanning, as of this writing, just over 25 years.

And no, Kaul and I hadn't the faintest intention in 1973, when we invented RAGBRAI, of creating the most successful newspaper promotion since William Randolph Hearst started the Spanish-American war. Indeed, our intentions were modest to the point of embarrassment: Our only goal was to talk *The Register* into paying our expenses while we tootled across the state on our bikes.

We also assumed it would be a one-time event, rather than what Kaul later called "a life sentence." We hadn't anticipated the incredible enthusiasm that the ride generated. Nor had we anticipated the wonderful hospitality of people throughout Iowa. But most of all, we hadn't anticipated Clarence Pickard of Indianola who, at age 83, became an inspiration to us all. More, much more, about him later.

The 1973 article continued: "We're going to ride rain or

shine, hot or cold. Each day's ride will leave at 8 a.m. except the hundred-miler to Williamsburg. See you in August."

I called that first ride the Great Six-Day Bicycle Ride Across Iowa. Kaul and I expected maybe a dozen or so people to show up in Sioux City, but as the date grew closer it became apparent that a lot more than that were going to join us. I'd had many letters and phone calls, but Kaul and I and my wife Ann still were astonished when we arrived in Sioux City to find something over 250 people ready to set out with us the next day.

As Don Benson, then of *The Register*'s promotion department remembers it, "We got to the motel and all of a sudden all these other people started showing up. Clarence Pickard was there. He'd gone up by bus and Bill Albright (of Bill's Cyclery) took his bike up."

Among those gathered there, besides Pickard, were the late Tom Hunt, retired president of Fairfield Aluminum Castings Co., who had trained diligently for the ride; then-Senator Dick Clark, better known for his earlier pre-election walk across Iowa, who rode only as far as Kingsley; Bill Wertzberger of Dubuque, who had cycled to Sioux City, camping along the way; and Sandy and Bob Tatge of Des Moines, already veteran touring cyclists, who also cycled to Sioux City from home.

I cannot emphasize too strongly the naivety of the planning that went into that first ride. There was, in effect, no planning, and what little there was was inept. First, everyone at *The Register*, including Kaul, Benson and me, thought of the event as no more than an elaborate joke and treated it accordingly.

Here is how Benson, who handled special events in the promotion department at the time, remembers the beginning.

You came in and talked to [department manager] Roy Follet or [managing editor] Ed Heins did. The next thing I knew Roy talked to me and said Karras and Kaul were going to ride their bikes across Iowa so Kaul could get some local color for his column.

Roy told me to take care of it. I told Roy it can't be too damned difficult to make two room reservations, and that's just about it. That's what we were talking about. We had the hot air balloon then, Craig Zevde and his assistant were to fly the balloon mornings and evenings in the overnight towns and he would carry your baggage, too.

I called and made the motel reservations, and then you and Ann and Mark, our son, and Kaul drove up to Sioux City. The route had not been driven ahead of time. You laid it out on maps. So we went up to Fort Dodge and picked up the route. We got on that county road just east of Storm Lake and the road was closed. A bridge was out. You had to take five miles of gravel around that bridge. You couldn't just go a mile north and a mile east. You had to go two miles north. It was RAGBRAI's first detour.

Benson also recalled that "we stayed in the Rodeway Inn. Two or three blocks from the hotel somebody had their first flat tire. There was absolutely no traffic. Anyway, we went to the airport and Mark and I flew back to Des Moines."

It was a truly rag-tag looking group that cycled out of Sioux City that Sunday morning in 1973. Kaul, Ann and I were the only ones in bike shorts, bike shoes and jerseys. We also were the only ones wearing helmets—those old leather-strap racing affairs that offered almost no protection. There were no other bicycle helmets at that time.

Almost everyone else was wearing cutoffs, gym shorts, walking shorts or bathing suits, T-shirts or tank tops and sneakers. All the neat cycling apparel came on the market later.

To compound our errors, we had an official (and stupid)

5

starting time of 8 a.m. every day except Thursday, the day of the 100-mile ride from Des Moines to Williamsburg, when the official starting time was 7 a.m. The stupidity lay in our expecting and wanting people to observe any official starting time (I can call it stupid because it was my idea). As we learned in later years, the best thing we could hope for was that everyone would start at different times.

The towns that year were chosen without consulting any townspeople. We made no provision for bike repair, medical help, traffic control, or for any conceivable emergency that might arise. Indeed, it's an even chance that the bikes might not have gotten very far out of Sioux City if it hadn't been for Bill Albright, then owner of Bill's Cyclery in Des Moines. He wanted to do the ride, so brought along a 12-foot trailer, $5,000 worth of spare parts (including 50 tires), the required tools, and sat outside his motel room every night repairing the bikes that had broken down during the day. As it was, the absence of planning kept showing up in minor crises throughout the week.

One thing we did right without even knowing it was schedule the ride the last week of August. That kept the number of riders down because all the schools in Iowa except those in Des Moines were in session (and boy, did I hear about that. I got dozens and dozens of letters from teachers and teenagers telling us to schedule the event the next year before school started so they could attend).

I don't know what we would have done if a couple of thousand riders had greeted us in Sioux City. Turned pale at best, snuck away under cover of darkness at worst.

From Sioux City the ride overnighted in Storm Lake, Fort Dodge, Ames, Des Moines and Williamsburg before ending in Davenport.

Sandra Tatge remembers that about 30 riders camped each night the first year. The second year, she said, there were at least 1,000 camping along the way. She also remembers that when she and Bob arrived in Sioux City they sought me out and asked about camping facilities. She says I arranged for them to stay at city and county parks, but I have no idea how I did that, if I did.

Benson arranged camping at the Naval Reserve Center lawn at Fort Des Moines. The building was kept open all night for showers and bathrooms.

Ann's and my lasting impressions of that first year's ride include extreme heat, endless hills, brutal headwinds, anticipation, Ann getting lost in a small town, exhilaration and chaos. Looking through clippings from the time, however, I see that only the first three days were beastly hot and the headwinds let up after the third day.

As for the last item in that list, chaos, it surrounded us every day. Item: one evening as I sat in the motel room banging out the next day's story on my old Smith-Corona portable there came a knock on the door. "I can't find my little brother," said a small voice. Kaul chased out into the night to help him, and I sent Ann to interview Clarence Pickard without pencil, paper or suggestions. Another time whoever was at the door couldn't find his sleeping bag.

Then there was the appalling task of dictating the story in a loud voice over the phone to whoever answered on *The Register*'s city desk. If you've never had to read your priceless words aloud in the presence of skeptical and wiseass colleagues you haven't lived. Invariably, I'd read an obviously clumsy sentence and someone in the corner of the room would call out, "Great line" to the laughter of everyone else. Several times I recruited Ann to dictate the story so I could avoid the comments.

But life does and did go on.

The official high temperature the first day, Sioux City to Storm Lake, was 99 degrees, but there's no doubt in the minds of those who were there that the temperatures were well over 100 degrees in some spots out on the road. But the hospitality along the way more than made up for our discomfort.

In my *Register* story for that day I wrote: "Perhaps the most pleasant aspect of the day was the enthusiasm for the project shown by those along the way."

Dwight and Joyce Rawson of rural Kingsley had free cold lemonade for the riders. They said their daughter had recently done a long bike tour and had told them how welcome a cold glass of lemonade was to a hot and thirsty cyclist.

And the Rawsons were not the only ones. There were also welcoming committees and escorts. Plymouth County Sheriff Ed Guntren and State Trooper William Wruck greeted bikes at the Plymouth-Woodbury County line, then, realizing how strung out the procession was, patrolled the route until all the bikes had passed.

The town of Kingsley went all out at the urging of Mayor Jim Watkins. As the riders straggled into Kingsley townsfolk and business people greeted them with smiles and handshakes. Pop, coffee, sandwiches and donuts were provided in the air-conditioned Brookside Golf Clubhouse compliments of Kingsley.

In his Over-the-Coffee column, Kaul wrote: "Most places one goes nowadays, they throw rocks at strangers, not a warm welcome like this."

There were others. Guy and Kay Brown of Pierson used the farm home of Mrs. Brown's father, R. J. Irwin, to set up a lemonade and cookie stand. There also were refreshments at Brown's Trading Post between Kingsley and Washta. And Bonnie Biller of rural Cherokee filled water bottles and invited the riders to take a dip in her backyard pool, which many of them did, clothes and all.

Many of the riders were able to ride only the first day because they had to get back home Monday for work or school. Doug and Kris Meinhard, for example, drove all the way to Sioux City from their home in Newton to ride the first day. And they took turns carrying their sons, Troy, 3, and Matt, 18 months, on their bikes.

The Dean Linn family of Fort Dodge, on the other hand, took a week's vacation to do the ride. Dean, 48, Nina, 46, Cindy, 16, and Larry, 14, took turns riding and driving their camper.

What Ann remembers of the end of that day is Kaul flopping on a bed in the brand new motel without screens, me whipping a blanket around like a toreador trying to chase out flies, and Ann watching in dazed exhaustion as the two heroes behaved like idiots.

The second day's ride from Storm Lake to Fort Dodge was just as hot as the first. Kaul wrote in his column:

> Another day, another 65 miles, another 95 degrees. Who ordered the weather for this bike trip anyway? Lawrence of Arabia?
>
> All over Iowa, schools are dismissing classes because of the heat. Football teams are cutting short practice sessions because of the heat
>
> Simultaneously, more than 200 mad bikers are struggling their way across Iowa in that same blazing heat because it's their idea of a good time.
>
> And it has been a good time ... largely because of the people on the trip and along the route.

He wrote specifically about Gene Angove, 61, a former carpenter who then was farming near Knoxville. Why was he doing this madcap stunt?

"One, I think I'm getting a little childish," he told Kaul.

"Two, I have a heart condition and I wanted to see if I couldn't strengthen my heart up a little.

"Three, I was the worst driver in the world. I used to come up behind people on bicycles and honk my horn and wonder why they wouldn't get out of the way. I wanted to come on this trip and see who was right and who was wrong. It turns out I was wrong."

There were just 12 women on the first ride and when asked why they came some of the comments were:

Pat Bjorklund of Renwick: "Just for the fun of it. I wanted to do it but everyone said I couldn't."

Liz Garst of Coon Rapids said, "I've been working on my father's farm this summer, riding a horse and cutting out cows for breeding. I'm a cowboy. I'm here because I'm a great fan of Donald Kaul."

Leann Olson, 20, Milford, said that when a motorist shouted at her, "Having fun?" she responded, "I have to. It's my vacation."

Elise Jensen of Newell, 48, read about the tour and thought, "Oh, would I like to try that." She rode one day, from Storm Lake to Fort Dodge. Her mother had given up bicycling three years earlier, at age 80.

Ann got the week off at the last minute and did it for the same reason as so many other women. "My husband said I couldn't make it, so I had to prove I could," she says.

And there were other reasons.

Jim Kollmann, 18, of Iowa Falls, said, "I think it's because I'm stupid."

Chuck Thiede, 15, Storm Lake, said "I'm not very good at athletics and I wanted to prove I could do something besides classroom work." He was excused from school for the week to go on the ride.

Three Newton High School students also were excused from school to do the ride. The principal, Robert Bennett, said they'd probably get more out of the experience than they would from the first week of school. The three were Marty Doane, Clark Johnson and Robert Dixon, all 16. Doane now operates bike shops in Newton and Pella.

The hospitality continued unabated.

Art Schraeder gave away soda pop at his DX station in Varina; school was let out at Varina to let students ride a little of the way; and free pop and cookies were handed out at Clare Mayor Carl Donahoe's grocery store.

About that time, someone at *The Register* got in touch with the most famous odds maker in America, Jimmy (the Greek) Snyder and asked what the odds were that Kaul and I would make it to Davenport without mishap or without quitting. He pondered that for a while, and called it at four to one.

No provisions for camping had been made in Fort Dodge, so the campers sought and received permission to put up their tents on the grassy areas around the Best Western Starlight Motel, where the rest of the riders were staying. And when Mrs. Tatge climbed out of her tent to tell the management that the campers (who were charged nothing, by the way) were having trouble getting to sleep because of the outdoor security lights, the management without a peep of protest turned them off.

The third day's ride from Fort Dodge to Ames was also blistering hot, but with a pleasant cooling break in the sandstone canyon of Dolliver Memorial Park south of Fort Dodge. We rode through water at the park's one ford and enjoyed the shade.

The hospitality, of course, went on and on.

Ching Williams, operator of the Clover Farm Store in Lehigh, passed out pop and chocolate milk, and the Golden Memories Club, a senior citizens group, gave away home-baked cookies.

Several members of the Stratford High School girls' basketball team were out on the road to greet Kaul, who was famous throughout the state for his snide comments about three-on-three girls' basketball. The young women, chanting school cheers, escorted him into town and had him autograph a basketball.

In Boone, members of the Boone Bicycle Club escorted riders to City Hall, where they were treated to home-grown tomatoes and lemonade. In my *Register* story the next day I wrote that "never did a tomato taste so good."

The best trick of the day, however, was pulled by Mr. and Mrs. Donald Rossiter of Moneta, on their way to Ames to pick up their son, Dennis, who had ridden from Sioux City.

Kaul and I, both very hot and very tired, were riding together south, just the two of us on the road (a rarity even the first year), on County Road R 27 when a car shot passed us and came to a stop at a gravel road several hundred yards away. A man jumped out, threw open the trunk and busied himself with something or other. When we pulled up to see what was going on, he handed each of us half of a juicy, home-grown cantaloupe.

It was Don Rossiter. Kaul and I just buried our faces in the cantaloupe.

Near the end of the day several incredibly stupid riders (it still embarrasses me to admit that the two ride leaders were among them) cut off 10 miles by braving the high-speed traffic (including many heedless semis) on U.S. Highway 30. That marked the beginning of ill-advised shortcuts, a practice that still continues, fortunately rarely. And, incidentally, the leaders never knowingly did that again.

From Ames we rode the next day to Des Moines, a day marked for the first time in the week by frustrating officiousness and terrifying traffic.

The distance was 43 miles by the bike route roads, and at least 400 other bicyclists joined just for the day, which finally turned relatively nice with temperatures under 95 degrees for the first time that week.

The ride went well from Ames south through Slater, Sheldahl and Polk City. In Slater, the riders were plied with refreshments by Beta Sigma Phi, a social sorority, which had expected no more than 40 riders. After the first wave hit, the women were hard pressed to mix lemonade fast enough.

In Sheldahl, the school children were out on the street greeting the cyclists, and in Polk City, the bank served lemonade and cookies.

Things started to get sticky at the intersection with the main highway into Des Moines. Intentions were good, but the execution flawed. A Polk County deputy sheriff was stationed at the intersection to escort the cyclists into Des Moines, and he was

12

determined not to let us proceed until all of us were assembled.

We stood there waiting in the blazing sunshine for what felt like three hours, but probably was no more than half an hour, when he finally agreed to start out.

The police escort was fine for those riders at the front of the line, but the line fractured at intersections and traffic lights, and those left behind were left without any protection.

Those of us in the back battled the terror of Fleur Drive with its many sewer gratings (arranged parallel to the street and guaranteed to catch a wheel and throw the rider) and even worse, angry motorists who had been held up by the front of the line of cyclists.

However, there was some compensation. Each cyclist was given a rose by a local florist, but the question was, how did one carry it? Obviously, in your hand with the blossom drooping into the front wheel where it was promptly severed from the stem.

Nevertheless, all the cyclists got to Des Moines one way or another. There had been a minor bike-car accident in Ames but nothing untoward happened in Des Moines. *Register* and *Tribune* salesmen were on hand at the Hyatt House to greet the riders. All was rather magical that evening outdoors in the lamplight.

Everyone was enjoying the calm before the 100-mile day from Des Moines to Williamsburg. Almost everyone also was full of anxiety about the next day. Remember, the year was 1973, long before century rides became commonplace and routine. Riding a bike 100 miles in one day was still a big deal. There also was the question of the weather. How could any of us survive 100 miles if the heat didn't break?

As it turned out, that day was cool and beautiful. I wrote in my *Register* story for that day that the ride really began for me "three miles east of Prairie City, where a paved county road takes off due east from Iowa Highway 163."

It was there that the ride became biking as I've come to know and love it in Iowa—lush, rolling farmland, the valleys in the distance lost in a soft blue haze; a wide road with light traffic; a cool snappy breeze from the south (a west wind would have been preferable).

The other days of the Great Six-Day Bike Trip have been good. The countryside has been lovely, the people wonderful and the weather delightful—in air-conditioned rooms.

But Thursday was great, and on that stretch east of Prairie City it was greatest.

If any legislators suggested now that "beautiful land" be put on Iowa's automobile license plates, I would not snicker as I once did.

And yet again, the cyclists were plied with refreshments and cheered on all along the route—by the students at Prairie City Community Schools, by girls' basketball players in Montezuma, by a group of women serving lemonade in Deep River, and by the Chamber of Commerce and the Latona Players, a drama group, in Williamsburg.

Kaul and I stayed in a family home in Williamsburg, something that I had set up weeks before, while Ann went to a motel. It was my notion that if we were going to stay in a small town we should at least meet someone who lived there and spend some time with them. As it turned out, Mrs. Arlene Eckhart and I sat up in her back yard talking and drinking beer until well past midnight. Kaul went to bed, but I had a delightful evening.

Mrs. Eckhart and her husband operated what was then known as the Little Chicago Cafe in Williamsburg. They also had a delightful daughter, Sharon, then 10, whom I gladly would have adopted.

Friday, from Williamsburg to Davenport, was the last day of the first ride. New riders continued to join in that day. And

Clarence Pickard, wearing his silver pith helmet, continued to bring people out. All the students in an elementary school in Iowa City lined the curb waiting for him, and cheered when he finally appeared.

Register staff writer Larry Eckholt wrote that Pickard had made the silver pith helmet a symbol of virility and longevity.

The Quad-Cities Bike Club and the Chamber of Commerce were on hand to greet the riders in Davenport. Kaul and I also were invested into the Order of the Tube by Henry Cutler, a friend of Kaul's. He presented us with inflated bike tubes laden with chrysanthemums and green ribbons.

By actual count, 114 bikers made the entire trip while at least 1,000 were in and out of the tour along the way.

How can I be sure of the count? Because at the last minute, in the Davenport park where we finished, it finally occurred to me that we'd made no provision for patches commemorating the ride.

And so, in a frenzy, I ran around collecting paper and pencils, yelled at everyone in the park to form four lines, and had the riders write down their names and addresses and pass the paper and pencil back to the next person.

We later had patches designed and made, and sent them to the 114. Ann and I still have ours.

Without question, it was a memorable week, one of the more memorable of my life. Indeed, it would be no exaggeration to say that it actually changed my life.

Don Kaul summarized the tour by saying, "It wasn't the heat; it wasn't the legs; it wasn't the risk of a breakdown. The real test," he said, "was how much a person's backside could endure sitting on the small bike saddle."

That was right on the mark, but the tour was a lot more than that. It was a coming of age for some people, a magnificent test passed for others, the fulfillment of dreams for yet others.

Besides, we had the constant diversion all week of news of the hearings chaired by Senator Sam Irvin of North Carolina into the break-in of Democratic headquarters at the building known as the Watergate.

The next year, during the second ride, we had the diversion of the first resignation of a president in modern times, that of Richard Nixon. But that's for a later chapter.

The 83-Year-Old
Wunderkind There is no question that the

late Clarence Pickard of Indianola, then 83, was the

overwhelming inspiration in 1973 for everyone on the first

RAGBRAI, called the Great Six-Day Bike Ride Across Iowa,

and for multitudes all across the state as well.

He literally became an Iowa legend in one week. By the time
the ride, which started in Sioux City, reached Davenport, children were being let out of school to stand by the roadside and
wait for him to come by. Just about everyone marveled at the accomplishment of the man.

Besides, he was the George Burns of cycling. He had everything: charm, a disarming humility, age, seeming frailty, a lively
sense of humor and a seemingly naive faith that somehow or
other, against all odds, he would be taken care of. One was reminded of that pathetic line by Blanche DuBois in *A Streetcar
Named Desire*: "I have always depended on the kindness of
strangers."

Consider, he came to Sioux city the last week in August by
himself, having made no arrangements for housing or camping
or anything else. We found him, got him a motel room, made
sure he had something to eat and wondered how long he would
last.

I recall that someone, perhaps a photographer, had looked in
on him in his motel room and found him lying on his back

asleep, his hands folded on his chest. Concerned, the photographer urged Donald Kaul to take a look. "He looked dead," Kaul told me.

Then, later, when I talked to him I learned he'd bought a second-hand 10-speed women's model Schwinn Varsity, green as I recall, a bike that weighed somewhere between 30 and 40 pounds. "I never saw one of these bikes before this," he told me, but the people he talked to had pressed him into buying the 10-speed for a trip of this distance.

He hoped to ride the entire 410 miles, he said. Asked why he was doing this, he said, "It was just a fool idea I had." (Years later, during a visit I made to his home in Indianola, he admitted to me that he had had a much more serious purpose in mind: "I wanted to show that just because a person was up in years he could stay active and didn't have to just sit around in a rocker." He certainly accomplished that.)

He continued, "My wife is going into the hospital so I thought I'd take a vacation."

"How many miles have you trained, Mr. Pickard?" I asked.

"Oh, about half a block," he said.

"He'll never get out of Sioux City," I told Kaul, and Kaul agreed. Little did we know.

For frail little Clarence—he stood 5-feet-6 and weighed only 116 pounds—turned out to be a man of steel.

First, he rode at a glacial pace. It was very difficult to ride with him because he was so slow. But he rarely stopped. As Kaul mentioned more than once during the week, "I keep passing him and passing him, but he always finishes."

Second, he fell down a lot—several times a day, but never hurt himself. "I can tell when I'm going," he told me, "and I just look for a soft spot and just go down, then get myself up kind of easy."

Later in the week, while riding through Dolliver State Park, I discovered he hadn't learned how to shift gears properly. We were riding along together and I noticed that both gear levers

Donald Kaul and Clarence Pickard. Pickard, who was then 83, wore a pith helmet on the first ride in 1973.

Copyright 1973, the Des Moines Register and Tribune Company. Reprinted with permission.

were at the same angle. If you've ever ridden a 10-speed you know that the levers work in opposite directions for the purpose of shifting. Left lever back and right lever forward puts the bike in its highest gear; left lever forward and right back puts the bike in its lowest, or easiest, gear.

I told him, "We have a pretty big hill coming up, Mr. Pickard, and it looks to me like you're in a pretty high gear."

"Well," he said, "that's the way I've been doing it."

I then suggested that he push the left lever forward and pull the right lever back when he got to the hill. I saw him a short time later and he told me, "Say, I tried that on that hill back there and it really made a big difference."

I should think so. Being in the right gear for the terrain goes a long way to making all the difference.

In an interview later in the week with Chuck Offenburger, then a new reporter at *The Register* (he later started his Iowa Boy column and later still became co-host of RAGBRAI with me, but that, too, is for a later chapter), Pickard revealed his own "folksy thoughts about being 83 years old and doing something as crazy as riding a two-wheeler across Iowa."

Offenburger started the story, with italics above his byline, with a quote from Kaul: "By the end of the day, everyone's tired and hates each other. But the one thing that keeps you going is that long after you've quit riding, somewhere back there—still riding—is Mr. Pickard, and he's smiling. He's 83 years old and if he can make it, then, by God, the rest of us can, too."

Pickard told Offenburger: "I'm not all that phenomenal like people have been saying. It's just that I've always worked hard—farming, cutting trees, gathering trash—and I'm in good shape."

Offenburger wrote that there was no doubt in Pickard's mind that he could make it all the way to Davenport. "I go at my own pace and try to stay somewhere near the rest of them," Pickard said. He also told Offenburger that he ran half a mile every night at home in Indianola. "I do it because of something I read. And that is that older people should do some kind of exercise three times a week, or more often, that will bring the heart up to its full extension of effort.

"You want that heart to beat hard, but not for very long, so that it can get used to meeting emergencies—like catching a streetcar or heading off a hog—whatever the situation is."

Of his background, he said he was born in the Flint Hills of Kansas, moved to Iowa as a boy and was graduated from Simpson College in Indianola. He earned a master's degree in agronomy from Iowa State University in Ames and was involved in farming most of his life.

Early on, he said, he rode a bicycle from Indianola to Chillicothe, Mo., where he sold vacuum cleaners. "I was just testing myself," he said, "and I figured Chillicothe was far enough from home that if I made a booboo, not everyone in Indianola would know about it."

He and his wife, Mildred, also joined the Peace Corps in the late 1960s as two of the oldest volunteers ever, and served two years in India. Pickard told me years later that he believed one of the great accomplishments of his life was to persuade Hindus that they could eat eggs without fear of threatening any life if they just kept roosters out of the chicken yard. In the intervening years he worked first as an agricultural extension agent and later began active farming.

Pickard described his daily routine in detail for Offenburger, including a light breakfast—"I'll eat a half piece of toast, an egg and milk. We used to split a strip of bacon, but now that meat's gone so high we skip it." He said he started in on farm work right after breakfast, ate a light lunch and a rather hearty dinner, then read, relaxed, ran his half mile and got to bed between midnight and 1:30 a.m.

His attire on the ride had become the subject of much comment and speculation. Despite the brutal heat of the week, Pickard had appeared every day in long-sleeved shirt, full-length trousers, high-top tennis shoes and a pith helmet. He revealed to Offenburger a further secret of his clothing—a white wool sweater that he wore under his shirt.

"Now the reason I wear it," he told Offenburger, "is that the sun goes beyond the outer garment, and if the heat of the sun can get to your skin without insulation, then your blood temperature will rise, and this will be manifested in what's happening to many of these kids—they get all poohed out. I stay insulated and cool."

Since Pickard seemed to do so well with wool clothing, Ann decided to try a wool shirt on the short ride from Ames to Des Moines that first year. She said later that "it was as close to heat exhaustion as I've ever been."

He also talked about the frugality of the life that he and Mildred had lived, saying that they neither smoked nor drank nor had any other expensive habits. "And I am married to a woman," he continued, "whose good looks are so durable that she has never found it necessary to go to a beauty shop."

The interview was done the day the ride arrived in Des Moines, the day before the 100-mile route to Williamsburg, a day all of us feared. Pickard said in the interview, "I guess I might have to put my lights on before I get there."

And get there he did, at about 8 p.m., but not without mishap. He took a wrong turn at Colfax and wound up pedaling along on the shoulder of Interstate 80.

"Well, heck," he said in a *Register* story by then staff writer Michael Wegner, "we were supposed to go east but I came to a point where Highway 6 turned north so I turned off on I-80— it was the nicest track, all macadamized—and I figured that on this road I'll be in Williamsburg by noon."

Frank Fisher, a state trooper who later served several years as RAGBRAI safety coordinator, stopped Pickard and told him it was illegal to ride a bike on I-80. "You get me out of here but quick," said Pickard, who referred to Fisher in Wegner's story as "a crusty little fellow."

Pickard was given a ride back to the official route at Sully and finished the day without further incident.

As I mentioned earlier, all the students at an elementary school in Iowa City were let out to stand along the street and wait for Pickard to come through. When they saw him they began cheering and applauding. Pickard came to a stop—and promptly fell down. But gracious man that he was, he picked himself up, swept off his pith helmet and went into a deep bow. The kids went wild.

At the end of the ride, in Vander Veer Park, Pickard was presented with a "Senior Citizen of the Day" certificate by Mayor Kathryn Kirschbaum. He rolled up the certificate, stuck it in his shirt pocket and proceeded with the business of signing autographs, shaking hands and answering questions.

In his late 80s, he and Mildred moved into a retirement home in Indianola. Pickard died at age 92 in the winter of 1982 after being struck by a car one night as he walked across a highway.

My wife and I went to his funeral in Indianola. I was shocked to see that hardly anyone attended, but as someone explained, he had outlived all his friends.

We dedicated the next year's RAGBRAI to his memory, calling it the Clarence Pickard Memorial Ride. Fittingly, that year's RAGBRAI patch was generally in the shape of a pith helmet.

Before the Beginning— Stirrings of a Belated Youth

Donald Kaul, Ann and I came to serious cycling (she because of my wheedling to join me) in the late 1960s and early 1970s, and it literally changed our lives. Looking back now, I suspect it was our benign substitute for the often disruptive and wrenching mid-life crisis (divorce, anxiety, recriminations). Or perhaps it *was* our mid-life crisis. Whatever, our experience was without a doubt an example of how an essentially trivial (if not outright childish) enter-prise can result in profound change.

It was an exciting time for us, a journey of discovery and just a barrel of fun besides. We were hardly kids at the time—my wife and I were in our late 30s and early 40s, Kaul in his middle and late 30s. We were responsibly employed and married with chil-dren—but I would be less than truthful if I didn't tell you that one of its great appeals was that cycling made us feel like kids again.

Today, everybody (or so it seems) cycles, but in those years almost all the people on bicycles were children. There were hardly any serious cyclists in Iowa, or in the United States for that matter. In Iowa, all the long-distance cyclists knew each other by their first names, and Kaul and I didn't know any of them. Ignorantly, we thought we were pioneers, which made the experience even more intriguing.

We had biked as kids, Ann in Maplewood, New Jersey, I in Cleveland, Ohio, and Kaul in Detroit, Michigan, but not as adults. Then in the early 1960s after joining *The Register* (and after President Eisenhower's physician recommended that everyone bike for good health) I started riding a three-speed bike to work with a *Register* colleague.

I enjoyed it so much I eventually got Ann and our three older kids on three-speeds and we'd all take occasional family rides. This was in the middle '60s. Our annual big excursion each summer was a ride to a huge public swimming pool at Camp Dodge, a National Guard training camp north of Des Moines. It was all of 15 miles, round trip, and most of our friends were astonished that we would even attempt cycling that far.

But it wasn't until 1967 that I even thought about long-distance cycling. I had lusted after a 10-speed bike for several years, exclaiming whenever I saw one on the street, and finally bought one in 1967, a brand new reddish-orange Raleigh Carleton for $125. Its components (brakes, derailleurs, cranks, pedals) are now considered obsolete, and justifiably so, but at the time it was simply an extraordinary beauty.

I'll never forget my first ride on that bike. I wheeled it out of the bike shop onto the sidewalk, got on, and turned the pedals around once. The bike and I coasted, and coasted, and coasted, and I thought, "I'm never going to have to pedal this thing." It was an epiphany. I was hooked. At that moment, without even a glimmer of insight into what was happening to me, I became a long-distance cyclist.

Kaul had been hired in 1960 as a reporter on the old *Des Moines Tribune* (which perished, along with most afternoon newspapers in the middle 1980s, alas) and he and I already had

26

Donald Kaul (left) *and John Karras, mid-1980s.*
Ann Karras photos

become pretty good friends by the time I acquired the Carleton. He also had become *The Register*'s Over-the-Coffee columnist and was crafting a wide and controversial reputation for himself in Iowa as an iconoclast, but funny. He never hesitated to satirize Iowa's most sacred institutions, and chief among them, girls' basketball.

Kaul and I had a lot in common. We had grown up under similar circumstances—in big, ugly industrial cities, under the influence of dominant females (I'm not going to go into that)— and were both (can I put it gently? no) essentially wiseasses. We hit it off almost from the moment we met, recognizing each other as kindred spirits.

Of course, after buying the Carleton, I assailed him with tales of the incredible joy of riding that bike. Within a year, he had bought a 10-speed, our wives—Ann and Sue—had bought 10-speeds and the four of us were out exploring the countryside near Des Moines.

Ann and I had a Volkswagen bus at the time, and with the middle seat out, we could get four bikes and four people into it. At least twice a week in those summers in the late 1960s, the four of us would pile in with our bikes and drive to Polk City, about 13 miles north of Des Moines.

We had two rides we'd take out of town, a 13-mile loop or a 12-mile out-and-back. Neither included any serious hills, but there were hills nevertheless. In a car you didn't even notice them. Just a little more pressure on the accelerator. On a bike, we huffed and puffed. I remember cycling along one time and hearing Kaul exclaim, "I never knew that hill was there."

What struck us first in those early rides was the beauty of the Iowa countryside when seen from a bicycle seat. The four of us had lived in Iowa for several years by then, had driven various places, had appreciated the spectacular views of the Northeastern Iowa hills, but had not been impressed by the area around Des Moines.

In a car, it was mostly corn and beans, not boring, exactly, but certainly not spectacular. True, in summer the state is pretty even in its flattest reaches because of its greenness and gently rolling fields, but again, hardly anything to exclaim over.

On a bike at 10 miles an hour, however, it was WOW!

The more we rode, the more we wanted to ride. Kaul took to scouting possible routes in his car and telling me about them. Then, when time was available, we'd go out and ride them.

What I remember as our earliest such ride was a route that took us from the Karras house on 44th Street in Des Moines through West Des Moines on Ashworth Road to where it ends in a T-intersection well into Dallas County (in those days, past Valley High School was out in the country), then south to Booneville and back into West Des Moines on Grand Avenue and into Des Moines on side streets to 44th Street.

Not only was it the longest ride we had attempted at that point, it also was the hilliest. Ashworth Road is a series of ups and downs with a killer hill at the end. Then, turning south toward Booneville, one faces four daunting hills, one after the other and each hidden from view until you top the one before.

Many oaths (most of them mine) turned the air blue on that ride.

We finished the ride close to exhaustion. "That had to be 40 miles," I remember saying.

"At least 50," Kaul said.

"Fifty-five," I said.

I later measured it in a car with a relatively accurate odometer, and the route topped out at almost exactly 30 miles.

But such excursions just whetted our appetites for more. You have to understand that neither of us ever had been an athlete, high school or college. The closest I ever got was going out for track in ninth grade, a pointless if not disastrous ambition for someone who was slow afoot and also couldn't jump worth a darn. I'm pretty sure that Kaul's forays into athletics were confined to following the futile efforts of the Detroit Tigers.

We also smoked, I from the age of 13, Kaul from college or shortly before. And we continued to smoke into the early years of RAGBRAI. But for me, that's another story.

The point is that we were unprepared for the changes that cycling was doing to us, namely, getting us in shape. We found the hills getting easier. We found the distances seemingly getting shorter. What was exhausting one week seemed feasible a month later. It was an exciting time for both of us. We were breaking new ground. We were becoming athletes. Not competitive athletes, but athletes all the same.

We did variations of the Ashworth Road ride, turning right at the T and riding into Waukee. That, including breakfast at the cafe in Waukee, became a favorite ride with west-side Des Moines cyclists for many years.

While Don and I were riding to work almost daily, Ann found a friend, Avonelle Moss, who enjoyed cycling to Waukee for breakfast. Several mornings a week they would cycle out, talking about family problems and joys. Ann put in a lot of miles on her bike every summer for many years that way.

29

For Kaul and me, though, two efforts stand out in memory as beacons in our cycling development. The first was a ride to Ames and back, the second a ride to Iowa City. Both were productions involving other people, our wives and other friends. In both instances, Kaul had scouted our routes in his car.

Kaul, Ann and I rode to Ames on country roads to Polk City, then north through Slater and Sheldahl into the western end of Ames. There, on the grass under the water tower north of Lincoln Way, Kaul's wife, Sue, met us with a picnic lunch. Ann drove back with Sue, and Kaul and I cycled back, a total distance of 75 miles. Once again, we finished exhausted but pleased as we could be at having actually covered that much distance on our bikes. I think that was the summer of 1970.

The Iowa City ride was much more elaborate and complicated, involving much arranging and coordinating. This was the plan:

Five of us would cycle from 44th Street to Iowa City: Kaul, my son Paul, his friend Paul Meintel, our friend and colleague George Anthan (who, by the way, had been a dedicated cyclist since boyhood) and I. My wife, Ann, would drive our Volkswagen bus with her bike inside to Williamsburg, then cycle the 25 miles from there to the home of our friends, Jack and Elaine Magarrell, in Iowa City. Jack Magarrell, meanwhile, who was in training for long-distance hiking, would walk the 25 miles to Williamsburg and drive the VW back to Iowa City. Once there and having dined, the five cyclists and Ann would pack into the VW and drive back to Des Moines. (I don't remember what we did with our bikes, because they certainly didn't fit inside the bus with the bunch of dead bodies in there on the return trip. As Ann remembers it, only Kaul and I drove back with her and the others made other arrangements to return to Des Moines.)

The ride was 125 miles, out of Des Moines on University Avenue through Prairie City to County Road F62 and then due east through Reasnor, Sully, Lynville, Searsboro, Montezuma,

Deep River, Millersburg and Williamsburg to Iowa City. I remember it as having taken us 13 hours, but suspect it was longer. I know our son, talking with me about that day years later commented that "it took forever."

Kaul and I had been reading everything we could find relating to long-distance cycling—how to train, what to eat, how often to take breaks, what to drink and on and on. A lot of the information was ill-guided or just plain wrong. Much of it came out of one nutritional fad or another. But no matter. We followed much of it anyway. We stopped every hour and walked the bikes for five minutes. We monitored our water intake. We snacked on the five pounds of gorp I had mixed up for the trip.

31

I remember being in a restaurant in Lynville for lunch. Anthan ordered a hamburger, and I immediately told him that meat was definitely not recommended for long-distance rides.

"Oh, okay," he said, and changed his order to a grilled-cheese sandwich. A few minutes later the waiter asked me what I wanted. "A hamburger," I said without thinking. Anthan yelled something at me, and I quickly switched to grilled cheese.

We met Ann and Jack Magarrell in Williamsburg and had snacks together at the Little Chicago Cafe (I have never tasted a better chocolate milk shake) before cycling on into Iowa City. We were dead by the end. It had been a beautiful day. A thrilling day, but we were dead. Being chased by a couple of dogs along the way had taken its toll. The hills had taken their toll. The distance had taken its toll.

But we had done it, ridden more than 100 miles in one day. And on that day (I think it was in the summer of 1971) the idea for RAGBRAI was born. Hell, we said, if we can ride to Iowa City in one day, why not across the whole state in a week? Not that we had a plan or even a proposal. At first blush, the idea seemed outrageous.

Our first proposal to our bosses was to send Kaul around the state the next summer as a representative of *The Register* to participate in the popular fund-raising bike rides, with *The Register* contributing so many dollars for each mile he rode. Everyone, including Kaul, liked the idea, but it never happened because he moved to Washington, D.C., in February of 1972 and what with the move and other complications, arrangements for the fund-raisers never were made.

Then he and I came up with the idea the next year, 1973, of a bike ride across the state, just the two of us, riding along and calling out to the local populace, "Hi, there, we're from *The Des Moines Register* and we're riding our bikes across Iowa just to let Iowans know that *The Register* really cares about all of you," or words to that effect, expecting to be greeted in return with the full range of Italian gestures. Our bosses wanted Kaul to ride it alone, but he said that was too dangerous and he wouldn't do it unless I came along. The company agreed, and a good thing, because Kaul had an alarming habit of forgetting where he was going and getting lost.

As I said, that was the plan, the whole plan. Modest to a fault.

It didn't take much to get it approved. It obviously was a low-budget promotional event, which pleased management, and *The Register* agreed to pay our expenses, which pleased us. In fact, that was our major goal in promoting the project.

Then, at almost the last minute (in June, actually) the then managing editor, Ed Heins, said to me, almost as an after-thought, "Why don't you invite the readers to come along?"

"Good idea," I said, not knowing whether it was or not. But you know how it turned out.

And that, dear friends, is how Kaul and I invented RAGBRAI.

The Second Year—We're Onto Something Big *The Register* has

decided to sponsor another cross-Iowa bike tour. ...

It will run again from the Missouri to the Mississippi, west to

east, to take advantage of whatever prevailing winds prevail.

Once again Donald Kaul and I will be token hosts and you're

all invited to ride the whole way or a mile or two.

The dates are Aug. 4-10.

That short piece—my announcement of what we came to call SAGBRAI (the Second Annual Great Bicycle Ride Across Iowa)—appeared in the Dec. 30, 1973, edition of *The Des Moines Register.*

I had no idea at the time what a watershed year it would turn out to be. What happened, in short, is that SAGBRAI, by the time it was over, shaped all the RAGBRAIs to come— as of this writing, 25 of them with a 26th on the way.

First and most important of all, Don Benson of *The Register*'s promotion department took over all the logistics of the ride, a job he juggled among all his other assignments as director of special events for 19 years. He is an organizing genius and a great detail man with an incredible memory. What he did, in brief, was impose order on chaos.

Second, the Iowa State Patrol got involved in the event as controllers of traffic safety, a relationship that has continued and expanded up to the present; and a relationship without which RAGBRAI would not be possible.

Third, we learned the hard way in trying to handle charter bus reservations (more on that later) to delegate everything we could to people outside *The Register.*

Fourth, we learned bit by bit that Donald Kaul and I had invented either a potential monster or one of the greatest Iowa entertainments and newspaper promotions in history (it has turned out to be some of each).

And finally, I learned more than I ever wanted to learn about depression (more on that later, also).

After the previous summer's first bike ride across Iowa, held the last week of August, I was inundated with letters from people wanting another ride. They wanted it held earlier, before school opened, so teachers and students could go. They wanted the dates announced in January at the latest so they could put in for vacation. But above all else, they wanted another ride. Hundreds and hundreds of them wanted another ride.

Obviously, we were onto something big.

And as soon as the announcement appeared on Dec. 30, people began writing to *The Register* for information.

In a January column, Kaul wrote, "People began asking for advice, more information, encouragement. Well, Karras handles the advice part of the trip, Don Benson hands out information and I handle encouragement," which aptly set the tone for all our roles. The letters poured in. The writers wanted information, reassurance, advice. Something obviously had to be done.

Early in the spring of 1974 I negotiated a deal with my boss, then managing editor Ed Heins, to write one article a week about SAGBRAI, about cycling, about getting in shape, whatever. I was working on the night copydesk at the time, an edit-

34

ing job, and was not officially a *Register* staff writer. I wanted Heins to pay me extra for the stories. He agreed to give me a day off from the copydesk instead. Deal.

The first piece, very short, appeared in *The Register* on my 44th birthday, March 10, 1974, for whatever that's worth, and asked readers who planned to attend SAGBRAI to write and let me know. In no time at all I had responses from 488 people, and the letters kept coming. In a story about the 448 I'd heard from, I asked readers to send in any questions they might have about cycling, the bike ride, "troubles with your teenager, hangnails, the trouble in Ethiopia. Anything at all."

The articles appeared each Sunday in the Iowa Living Section. I purposely adopted and maintained a flippant tone, for several reasons. First, I hoped to evoke a light, frivolous, relaxed tone for the event. Second, I wanted above all else to avoid pomposity (we were, after all, dealing with a bicycle ride, not a nuclear proliferation treaty). And third, like Kaul, I am and always have been at heart a wiseass.

For example, in an article that appeared in the May 12, 1974, *Sunday Register* I wrote these paragraphs under the subheadline Attitude:

> As I've been trying to convey from the start, the basic approach to SAGBRAI must be one of cordial, informal, happy insanity.
>
> What do we do if we're out there on the road between nowhere and nowhere and it starts to rain? We'll probably get wet. And when the rain stops, if we haven't found shelter on a farmhouse porch or in a barn, we'll dry out.
>
> How many miles do we ride before stopping for meals and water? As many as we wish. In riding 60 or 70 miles a day, how long will it take? Just as long as it takes. Not a moment longer.

35

Flippant, frivolous, fluffy.

I wrote a lot of stuff—a piece about bike clubs around the state and how to join one if you wanted company while training for the big ride; a piece about how to avoid hurting yourself while getting in shape; a piece about the best advice at the time on nutrition and so on and so on. But the articles I liked the best then and now were the question-and-answer pieces. They were the most fun to write, and, from this perspective, even now the most fun to read.

Examples (as found by Ann in the clippings):

Q. Will you be listing a breakdown of the participants by how many are male, female, ages, etc.?
A good idea and eventually we'll probably get around to that.

Q. Will we be going through scenic and low-traffic areas?
Just you wait. You won't believe it.

Q. Will you accept gifts?
Nothing more valuable than 15 cents.

Q. Will we be restricted as to the weight we can take?
Only informally. You know, no refrigerators, stoves or color TVs.

Q. How about snacks? motels?
Yes and yes

Q. Will we be stopping for fishing?
Forget the fishing If you want to go biking, go biking.

Q. Do you supply the Ben-Gay?
Only for my own aging legs.

Q. Is there any provision made for repairs along the way?
Bill Albright, owner of Bill's Cyclery in Des Moines, again is planning to bring his repair van on the tour. He and his crew will be making repairs each evening. His van is stocked with tires, tubes and replacement parts.

Q. Can we stay at relatives' houses at certain stops on the trip? *You certainly may. Any place along the way you have a relative with whom you're on good terms.*

Q. (from a 17-year-old) How many girls are going to go? *First, most of us find that riding from 60 to 80 miles a day is exhausting; second, I don't know.*

Q. How old would you like the people to be? Is 14 old enough? *If the 14-year-old can make it, yes, If not, no.*

Q. Any suggestions on how to convince two lazy husbands they will be able to manage their lives without us for seven days? *Just let them find out. After it's all over they'll appreciate you more and be better persons for it.*

Q. My mother says that if I don't pass algebra I can't go on the bike ride. Can you tell me why you'd need algebra on a bike hike? *You've found a sympathetic ear. Having been a child once and a parent now, I have some acquaintance with both sides of your problem. Young people sometimes do not do their best in school and parents sometimes make pronouncements they wish they hadn't. About the only thing you can do if you can't pass algebra is wheedle. As for algebra itself, I never got along very well with it. In fact if it were not for the binomial theorem, I'd be an engineer now instead of a newspaper person.*

Q. Are there any other states that have a ride similar to SAGBRAI? *None that I know of. There are many other tours around the country, but none quite as disorganized as this one.*

Q. How do you pronounce SAGBRAI? *Any way you care to. I'm getting sick of that name, and since I made it up, I may just change it. Maybe not.*

Q. Is there any danger of this great thing getting out of hand because of the numbers? I'd hate to think there would never be a TAGBRAI.
I share your concern and only time will tell.

One questioner asked about the possibility of pooling transportation to Council Bluffs and back from Dubuque, and that was the start of the bus-charter fiasco, mentioned earlier. I replied that a tour company was offering a charter service from Des Moines and back to Des Moines at a nominal charge. "Reservations must be made by July 3. ... Make checks payable to Hawkeye Tours and send them to Don Benson at *The Register*."

What a horrendous mistake. Before it ended (and I never did learn how everything got straightened out) our benighted secretaries were turning down reservations for buses that had space, and accepting reservations for buses that were full.

When the smoke finally cleared, Benson and I agreed that from that moment forward we would put the name, address and phone number of anyone offering an acceptable RAGBRAI service in the newspaper, and have all inquiries directed there. Never again would we try to handle such arrangements.

We stuck to that approach on all questions, and it has worked very well.

Writing the articles was fun, but the process had its dark side for me. It had the effect of adding to, heightening and intensifying the anxiety that was a palpable part of the preparation for this second bike ride.

Understand, an event of this scope was brand-new to all of us. There were the intangibles. The unknowns. We knew by early spring in 1974 that a lot of people—we still didn't know how many—were going to attend SAGBRAI, and we worried. We worried a lot. What if the towns couldn't handle the people? What if they ran out of food? What about sanitation? What about water? What if someone was killed?

The last was the biggest worry of all. As the time for the ride grew ever closer the three of us—Benson, Kaul and I—grew more and more certain that with the number we anticipated on the road there was no way we were going to get from Council Bluffs to Dubuque without at least one cyclist struck down and killed by a car. How would we be able to live with that? What were the legal implications? How could we get out of this alive?

As the actual event grew nearer, the anxiety kept building and building without our consciously realizing it. None of us had handled a situation quite like this before, and it had a lot to do with the depression that we all experienced to some extent for months after the ride ended.

In an article a week before the ride's start, for example, I wrote that even though I'd been emphasizing the relaxed nature of SAGBRAI, "some discipline will be required when we start en masse each morning. The reason is that without some discipline, we will be knocking each other down in the process of getting out of town. In fact, the prospect of 2,000 or so people on bicycles starting out together on a tour has been giving me nightmares for several months."

As everyone knows, people under heavy stress act anything but cool and calm, and my stress level was very high. In short, I was crabby. Kaul complained all week, calling me "contentious." I denied it, but he was right.

There were a lot of reasons at the time for the outpouring of enthusiasm we were getting. People were planning vacations closer to home because of a looming energy crisis. The American public also was in the midst of yet another infatuation with diet and exercise, with bicycling holding a special appeal. And finally, the first bike ride across Iowa in 1973 (with Clarence Pickard's participation as an added attraction) had sounded like great fun, like something that everyone who was able should try.

The SAGBRAI route started in Council Bluffs and ended in Dubuque with Atlantic, Guthrie Center, Des Moines, Marshalltown, Waterloo and Monticello being the overnight towns.

When our *Register* crew finally arrived in Council Bluffs the afternoon of August fourth we found a scene that made my heart sink—the day was oppressively hot and the air in the camping area choked with dust. SAGBRAI was happening at the end of a drought. By the end of that day, an estimated 2,000 cyclists had congregated in the area to start the bike ride the next day.

Amusingly, however, almost everyone was making the short trek from the campground to the Missouri River to dip the rear wheels of their bikes into the water. Just a short time before, I had mentioned in an article that "Of course, the ride will begin with the traditional dipping of rear wheels in the Missouri and end with the dipping of front wheels in the Mississippi a week later." Well, that was pure balderdash. There was no such tradition. I had made it up out of whole cloth while writing the article, but here were a couple of thousand people doing it. And they continue to do it today. The creation of that instant tradition well may be the greatest accomplishment of my life. Some accomplishment, eh?

And it was there in Council Bluffs at that dusty campground that Benson and I first met State Trooper Bill Zenor. Benson met him first, and this is how:

> We got to the park in Council Bluffs early Saturday morning and already there were cars pulling in and they just kept coming and coming. The Marine Corps Reserve brought a Waterloo club in their trucks.
>
> We had one baggage truck. And we had a van. And we'd taken the YMCA bike club trailer and our machinist at *The Register* had rebuilt it to hold 12 bikes rather than the six it originally held. In that parking lot at the Howard Johnson I had some bike flags, and was trying to attach two of them on the bike trailer.
>
> It had a spring bracket at the bottom and I was messing around trying to undo a bolt and saying a few choice words, and this voice behind me said, "Why don't you just tape it

on," and I said, "Where in the hell were you when I needed you?"

I turned around and saw these shiny shoes and went right up and here was this trooper standing there—he looked big—and then he started laughing and that was the beginning of a long friendship with Bill Zenor.

But the people kept coming and coming. And as the day went on, it didn't slow down but it picked up because people were coming late Saturday afternoon. That night I woke up in a cold sweat and realized we weren't going to have enough baggage trucks.

Benson sent his wife, Jackie, and another associate chasing around Omaha the next morning looking for another truck. They finally found one, and one of the trucks had to make two trips every day. Jackie drove the sag wagon with the trailer and Benson rented another car to get around in.

Zenor was the first trooper attached to RAGBRAI. He has been back almost every year since, first as RAGBRAI safety coordinator for several years, then as one of several troopers handling traffic safety, and finally as an assistant first to Benson and then to his successor as RAGBRAI coordinator, Jim Green.

Everyone associated with RAGBRAI knows Zenor. Even that first year, he'd follow a group of riders up a hill and announce on his car's loudspeaker, "Watermelon at the top of the hill," whether there was any there or not.

Seeing a rider going off into a cornfield to heed the call of nature, Zenor would say over the loudspeaker for all the world to hear, "Watch out for the corn bears."

This is how the state patrol got involved, as Benson remembers it. Sometime in the fall of 1973, after the first ride, Lt. Robert Glenn of Ames, who headed the community service officer group in the state patrol, called Benson and asked how he could get the patrol involved.

Glenn already was a dedicated cyclist. He had ridden from Ames to Des Moines in the middle of the week of that first ride, and immediately saw the public relations potential for the patrol.

He asked me to come out to a community service officers meeting, probably at Post 1. He explained to the troopers what we were planning to do and said he'd like to have a trooper along each day.

He asked who would take the first day, and Zenor said that was his post, and he'd take that day. He was just a trooper to me. I didn't know Zenor from a spot on the wall. Then Glenn asked who would take the second day, and Zenor said he'd take the second day, too. It was still in his post.

Bob said he'd take the third day and the fourth, they were both in his district. Then Glenn told this other trooper the next day was in his post, and the trooper said he was going to be on vacation. Glenn said he didn't have the trooper's chit, and asked when he decided. "About two minutes ago," the trooper said.

Trooper Cal Wagner wasn't at the meeting, so Glenn said Wagner would take the last two days, which he more or less did.

That was the beginning of a relationship between RAGBRAI and the state patrol that has lasted to this day to the mutual benefit of both. RAGBRAI has benefitted enormously—without the cooperation of the state patrol, in fact, it could not be held.

The patrol also benefitted greatly, mainly in the early years. The nation's campuses were aflame in the early 1970s because of opposition to the Vietnam War and the reaction to the disclosures from the Watergate hearings.

Those were the days when young people were calling police officers pigs, the days of not trusting anyone under 30.

And here, on the bike ride, young people saw a state trooper stopping semis on U.S. Highway 30 to let bicycles cross. The youths were astonished. Police officers helping young people. The effect was stunning.

The ride began Aug. 4. The headline on Kaul's column that morning was, "SAGBRAI Crazies Start Trek Today," and his advice was to the point: "THERE WILL BE NO LOOTING AND PILLAGING" was the first part; "Cyclists, never trust a motorist. The last cyclist I know who trusted a motorist is now a hood ornament on a '67 Ford pickup," was the second. The riders must have paid heed, because no one on SAGBRAI became a hood ornament.

We had arranged for a mass start the next morning for the benefit of a film *The Register's* promotion department was shooting for most of the week. We learned the next morning that a mass start was the last thing SAGBRAI needed. It was close to a disaster. We were six abreast behind a police car leaving Council Bluffs on old U.S. Highway 6. I don't know where I was in the pack, but as far as I could see in front and behind there was nothing but people on bicycles filling that Council Bluffs street.

Kaul's O.T. Coffee column likened the first day to the beginning of *Gone With the Wind,* but instead of an infinity of stretchers of the wounded, he wrote, there were bicyclists as far as the eye could see.

It was a white-knuckle ride for most of the morning because not only were the bikes too close together for safety, most of the cyclists also didn't know how to ride—they weaved back and forth, they turned around to look behind them, they stopped and passed without signaling. I'm not sure how many accidents or minor injuries there were, but there had to be plenty.

To my amazement, the newspaper clippings from the time show that we actually had planned another mass start the next morning from Atlantic, but fortunately for everyone, the SAGBRAIers were too smart to pay attention to it and left whenever they were up and ready, averting a second near-disaster.

Needless to say, we never again planned a mass start. In fact, even though we perpetuated the myth of an official starting time for many years, we encouraged everyone to stagger their departures.

As nearly as we could figure, there were about 2,000 cyclists on SAGBRAI, but we never were sure of the precise number. Bob Ulm stood on a bridge over the Nishnabotna River outside Hancock the first day of SAGBRAI and counted riders from 8 a.m. until well into the afternoon, and came up with 1,997.

Don Kaul had a different version in his column the next morning.

> The official count they are putting out is something on the order of 2,000. Don't believe it. I have an unofficial count that is much more accurate.
>
> I spotted a young lady in a farmyard near Hancock sitting on a step ladder watching the bikers whiz by. She looked as though she'd been there some time.
>
> "How many do you think have been past?" I asked her.
>
> "Five million," she answered without a smile.

Kaul went on to say that the major difference between SAGBRAI and the ride the previous year was size. "Last year you could get off on your own fairly easily," he wrote. "This year, no way."

The weather, incidentally, had changed 180 degrees overnight from hot and muggy the Saturday before the ride to clear and cool with a following wind out of the west. Kaul claimed to have ordered the weather. "John Karras ordered the hills," he wrote.

That's pretty much the way it went all the years that we co-hosted the ride—he would claim credit for whatever went well and give me the credit for the rest, all in good fun and in the spirit of making something out of very little, of course.

The town of Atlantic was our first overnight stop on SAGBRAI.

The tents, most of them lightweight nylon in myriad colors, were spread out over a lovely, wooded city park, and looked absolutely gorgeous in the evening light. The hospitality in Atlantic must have been outstanding because the bike ride has overnighted there more times than in any other town.

The next day's ride from Atlantic to Guthrie Center had as its centerpiece the resignation of President Richard Nixon. Word of the resignation raced through the troupe of cyclists with the speed of light, or almost. The Senate Watergate hearings with their revelations of political chicanery and dirty tricks, and the subsequent trials of several of the Republican participants left the president facing the possibility of impeachment. Thus, the resignation.

"The general reaction of the riders," according to Kaul's column, was, "'How much farther to Guthrie Center?' When you're out on the open road with the cattle lowing ... the problems of Richard (the President) Nixon seem very far away, indeed."

Guthrie Center, with a population in 1974 of 1,800, was the smallest overnight town on SAGBRAI. Back in the planning phase of SAGBRAI with Benson and Kaul, I had argued for including a small town in the route as an experiment to see how well the ride would be accepted there and how well a town of that size could handle it. We had assumed from the outset a year earlier that only Iowa's larger communities, with their more extensive facilities— motels, parks, sewage treatment plants and so on—and staff, could handle a large event. Benson and Kaul agreed to the experiment, and Guthrie Center was the choice. As things turned out, it couldn't have been better.

It well could be argued that we discovered RAGBRAI there, because everyone, townspeople and bicyclists alike, had the time of their lives.

A sign at the edge of town set the tone of the visit. It said, "Be kind, you outnumber us two to one." The Voyager out on the edge of town sold beer for a nickel a glass. As one fellow said, "I found a quarter on the floor and got drunk with it."

45

And I wound up in a downtown tavern arm-wrestling city employee Dean Osen, who looked like he could break me in half with a flick of the wrist. As Kaul wrote in the next day's *Register*, "We couldn't convince old John that Dean was letting him win so we hauled him away before he announced he could whip any man in the house."

During the evening in Guthrie Center a light plane appeared, circled the campground and a parachute appeared in the sky. And written on the small parachute was "Air-mail letter for Gene Angove." A bottle was attached with a message inside.

After it was all over, Darwin Hughes, president of the Guthrie Center Chamber of Commerce, said he "heard nothing but good comments." The residents, he said, had been somewhat apprehensive at the prospect of being invaded by 2,000 bicycle riders, but there was no trouble.

Just the opposite. Because the town's motel space was scant, the Chamber had arranged for 160 or so cyclists to stay with families, Hughes said, and both families and cyclists were pleased as could be with the arrangement. That was the first time such arrangements were made, and the practice has continued in small towns up to today with as many as 800 cyclists staying with families or camping in back yards. Typically, the families show the cyclists the town, shower them, entertain them and form friendships that last for years.

From Guthrie Center, the ride moved on to Des Moines, Marshalltown and Waterloo. SAGBRAI made little impression in those cities, but the small towns along the way turned out in force to feed and water the cyclists. Parks department officials in the larger cities were surprised and pleased that the parks where the riders camped were left cleaner than before the cyclists arrived.

The 80-mile ride from Waterloo to Monticello was simply brutal. It began in the rain, and when the rain quit the wind came up in the cyclists' faces. At 6 p.m., at least half of the 2,000 cyclists, exhausted because of the headwind, were still somewhere out in the country. Bikers were very happy to see the welcome sign in Monticello. "Why did you build your town so far from Waterloo," wailed one.

For my part, I didn't get to Monticello until 5:30 p.m. Waiting for me were Sandy Langenberg, the town's SAGBRAI coordinator, and Mayor Jim Townsend. According to a story in the *Monticello Express*, they'd been waiting since 1:30 p.m. at the top of First Street Hill to give me the key to the city. I remember Mrs. Langenberg asking me, "Where have you been?" and I remember replying, "Riding my damn bike from Waterloo."

The *Express* story characterized me as "cranky," and I wouldn't dispute it. The story continued, "Recognizing Mrs. Langenberg as his telephone contact in Monticello over the past months, he gave her a good-natured hug and asked the mayor in an off-handed way who he was. The presentation of the key was made graciously, however."

Eventually the riders straggled in, quite a few on the sag wagon, but as evening wore on the restaurants filled up, riders went off to the Jones County Fair (with free passes from the town) and bicyclists looked forward to the last day's ride to Dubuque.

Three-fourths of the cyclists stayed at the swimming pool campgrounds. Mrs. Langenberg said she "went down the day after they left and there wasn't even a handful of trash to be picked up. It didn't look like they had been there at all." And she concluded that "after seeing these bikers in action I'd love to have them back next year."

The ride ended the next day in Eagle Point Park in Dubuque with most anticipating another bike ride the next year. Donald Kaul and I spent at least half an hour autographing leftover dayglow directional arrows that had been used to mark the route all week and handing them out to cyclists who were about to leave for home.

47

At the age of 44 I was suddenly being treated like a rock star and realizing why so many of them are destroyed by that kind of attention at too young an age. After all, I'd been around the block a few times and had not changed appreciably in the last 20 years except for having a pivotal role in the bike ride. This sudden celebrity, I realized, could be most damaging if one took it seriously.

And that's when I found myself staring over a precipice into the black hole of depression. The emotional buildup for SAGBRAI had been incredible. By the week of the ride itself I was stretched out emotionally like a piano string. Kaul kept telling me I should relax, that I was way too testy. There also was the incredible reception we received across the state, and, let's face it, the celebrity that Kaul and I enjoyed for that week among the cyclists. As Kaul remarked on a RAGBRAI several years later, "For one week of the year, I'm Frank Sinatra."

Then, the next morning, in Dubuque, it was over. Done. We went out of the motel to the van to go somewhere and someone said, "Who's driving?" and I said, "I'll drive," and my wife made some remark about my trying to do too much and the next moment I found myself back in the motel room sitting in a chair and sobbing uncontrollably.

I've had several low points in my life, and that was among the lowest. The black mood hung on for several months. I'm sure today that I've never been closer to clinical depression. It turned out to be a valuable lesson. I swore at the time that I'd never again let circumstances take charge of my life like that, and haven't.

Both Benson and Kaul suffered a letdown after SAGBRAI, but not, I'm certain, as severe as mine. Talking about it with me years later, Kaul said, "It was tough going back to being just a columnist," to which I replied, "It was even tougher going back to the night copydesk."

Years of Change, 1975–1979

The acronym, RAGBRAI, first appeared in print in the *Sunday Register*'s Iowa Living section on Jan. 5, 1975, in a brief story I wrote announcing that *The Register* had decided to sponsor another cross-Iowa bicycle ride, the third annual.

The acronym came about this way. The first ride was called simply the Great Six-Day Bicycle Ride Across Iowa. All of us assumed at the time that the first ride also would be the last. How wrong we were. Popular sentiment—in the form of a flood of mail to *The Register*—demanded at least a second ride, which was called the Second Annual Great Bicycle Ride Across Iowa, or SAGBRAI.

Again, the public response called for another and it became obvious by the third year that the event was going to have a much longer life than any of us had expected. This raised the prospect of a TAGBRAI and even a NAGBRAI.

Something, obviously, had to be done. So I determined to make up an acronym that could go the distance, whatever that distance turned out to be, by simply tacking Roman numerals on it in each succeeding year. Further, as noted in the introduction to this book, I wanted it to be so long and ludicrous that everyone would think of it as a good-natured joke (which didn't work, alas, people took it seriously).

And finally, Michael Gartner, then the editor of the Register and Tribune Company, suggested (actually, he told me to), "Get *The Register*'s name in it, for crying out loud." He might not have said, "for crying out loud," which I did.

The result in 1975 was the title we've used ever since: RAG-BRAI (the *Register*'s Annual Great Bicycle Ride Across Iowa) with a Roman numeral.

Looking back, the years 1975–1979 were years of tremendous growth and change for RAGBRAI. It got bigger every year, from about 500 riders on the peak day from Ames to Des Moines in 1973, to over 2,000 the second year, to more than 6,000 by 1979.

But even more importantly, it evolved and changed. Most of the potential disasters involved in moving a medium-sized city across a state on bicycles arose and were dealt with. New disasters and other changes have occurred since 1979, of course, and some of the problems have never been satisfactorily solved, but by that year the ride had become very close to what it is today.

We had no safety officers with us the first year. The second year three state troopers served as safety coordinators in their separate districts. By 1979, we had 13 state troopers, all safety education officers, plus the assistance of sheriff's departments, local police and regular road troopers working at major traffic intersections in the cities and the countryside all across the state.

Our medical crew the first year, which we had nothing to do with providing, consisted of two young women who either were in nurses' training or had become nurses. They were along driving a Chevy Suburban for Bill Albright of Bill's Cyclery in Des Moines. The second year, one ambulance, volunteered by the late Walt Gary who owned an ambulance service operating in Davis and Jefferson counties, accompanied the ride. By 1979, we had five rescue vehicles with us all week and were calling on local ambulance crews for help when necessary.

The first year, Albright was the only bike shop owner on the ride. He brought a small trailer full of parts and sat in front of his motel door every night until midnight repairing bikes. By 1979, fifteen shops had joined the ride with repair vehicles on the road and in the campgrounds, along with displays of merchandise.

As for the explosion in numbers in those years, early on, Don Benson, the head RAGBRAI organizer in *The Register*'s promotion department, and I spent hours worrying about and trying to figure out how to control the growth. We had nothing against growth, of course, but also had no idea how big the thing could get without self-destructing.

We had visions (and fears) of the possibility of thousands of bikers stranded in some small town without enough of the essentials necessary for survival—food, camping space, water, sanitary facilities, toilet paper.

We had visions of a bicycle pack so big that it could create its own gridlock. In our worst scenarios, there were riots, burnings in effigy, calls for our executions. Well, maybe not.

But we were concerned. And while we still wanted to preserve above all else the impression of spontaneity and lack of regimentation that we'd been able to maintain, we also found it necessary to whittle away just a little bit at the free-spirited, devil-may-care atmosphere that had marked the first two rides.

As it turned out, all of our worrying and planning went for naught, because at every turn, year after year, the RAGBRAI crazies found a way around our attempts to contain the beast. There is no limit, it seems, to human ingenuity in the course of getting what it wants.

In the Feb. 21, 1975, story announcing the route of RAGBRAI-III, for example, I wrote,

> Once again *The Register* will carry the riders' baggage ... but with a variation on last year's theme.
>
> We're going to limit the amount of baggage we'll carry.

Please understand, this is being done out of raw fear rather than meanness of spirit. We're afraid that if we don't do something to keep the number of riders within reason, the event will overwhelm itself.

The story went on to say that we would carry baggage for the first 2,500 who wrote in and requested baggage tags.

Then in April, I wrote, "If you haven't already sent for your baggage tickets for *The Register*'s Annual Great Bike Ride Across Iowa-III (RAGBRAI-III), they're all gone. The quota for 2,500 riders has been filled."

As if that did any good. The response was a flood of letters telling us not to worry about carrying the writers' baggage because they'd made arrangements with others to drive and transport their stuff. Our carefully crafted attempt to limit the number was circumvented almost as soon as it was announced.

The dates for RAGBRAI-III were Aug. 3–9. The route started in Hawarden and ended in Fort Madison with overnight stops along the way in Cherokee, Lake View, Boone, Newton, Sigourney and Mount Pleasant.

We were estimating early that spring that about 3,000 would show up in Hawarden with bicycles. The actual number turned out to be closer to 5,000. And what happened? Did the ride self-destruct? Did people go hungry? Did towns run out of toilet paper? Not at all. Every community along the entire route took everything in stride and by the time we reached Fort Madison most of the cyclists were talking about coming back the next year.

The major questions every year along the route are: How many are here? Is it bigger than last year? Is this the biggest one yet? Is it getting out of hand?

The answer to that last one is that since RAGBRAI never has been in hand there's little chance of its getting out.

I don't know how many times we tried, without success, to

get an accurate count. Benson would hire someone to stand on a bridge or at an intersection and count the riders as they came by. We'd get that figure, then find out someone else had been counting somewhere else and had come up with a completely different number.

By RAGBRAI-V numbers of participants were inspiring headlines such as, "Onawa's population more than doubles overnight." That same year, speculation was rife on the number of cyclists. Orval Spahn of Mapleton, sitting in a golf cart at the edge of town and welcoming riders, said he had heard there were between 2,000 and 5,000. Don Benson, of *The Register*'s promotion department, jokingly suggested, "There are 3,499 today, because one guy dropped out." Marty Doane of Newton was told that 7,500 had been counted. Quite a trick, because no one was counting.

We even stooped so low as to resort to threats in our futile efforts to hold down the numbers. In the spring before RAGBRAI-VII, I quoted Benson in a *Register* story as saying, "If you don't have a baggage tag you probably will not get into the campgrounds so don't plan on getting around the system by carrying your own baggage or having your mom carry it in the car."

Of course, no one's baggage ever was left behind because it lacked a tag. Nor was anyone who needed it refused help. And the baggage problem, which at one time seemed insoluble because of the growing number of riders, solved itself.

As I noted in a RAGBRAI story in 1978,

> For three years running, *The Register* used a semi-trailer truck and a straight truck to haul the riders' baggage from one overnight stop to another. This year, we brought along two semis and a straight truck. One of the semis was full Sunday from Sioux City to Storm Lake, the other had about a quarter of a load and the straight truck was empty. What happened to all that baggage? Are the riders bringing less along? Are

there fewer riders? Are riders getting slimmer and wearing smaller sizes? Do they plan on bathing more frequently? Less frequently? Not at all?

What actually had happened was that the many clubs and teams that attend RAGBRAI had realized that the members could find their baggage more conveniently and quicker if the club rented a truck and hauled its own stuff from town to town. *The Register*'s baggage trucks unload all their cargo in one spot in the campgrounds, and in the early years it was a common sight to see cyclists wandering pathetically around and through that pile of luggage looking for their gear.

The 1978 ride marked the start of what has grown into a horde of support vehicles—baggage trucks, cars, campers—that follow RAGBRAI across the state. We even map, print and distribute an alternate route for them in order to keep cyclists and vehicles as far apart as possible.

Benson instituted the special vehicle route as soon as the support vehicles became numerous enough to be a problem on the bike route. That action was part of our over-all concern with the safety of the ride, beginning with the second year (the first year we were too dumb to be concerned about much of anything).

Every spring, beginning in 1974, I've written about commonsense safety on a bike. Cycling is, after all, a dangerous activity with perils most people are unaware of lurking around every bend: the parked car door that opens at the last minute in front of you just as you move out to go around the car; a sewer grating waiting to eat your wheel; the rear wheel of the bike in front of you, which, if you touch it with your front wheel, will fling you to the ground before you can blink an eye.

I have been urging safe practices upon the multitudes for years and years. Of course, the original rule of RAGBRAI was that there were no rules. The real reason for that stance was that we knew there was no way we could enforce rules if we tried to make any.

But suggestions were permitted, and I made them as force-fully as I could, even the second year. The week before the ride began, I wrote:

> As you know, SAGBRAI has developed as a rather infor-mal, unstructured ... escapade. Some discipline, however, will be required ...
> This is what the discipline involves: Everyone has to stay in line until we get out into the country. ... There are a few other common-sense rules that we all should observe. ...
> Riding in the oncoming lane of traffic is suicidal. Don't do it. If for any reason you have to stop, get your bike completely off the road. ... Do not make a left turn without looking be-hind you. ... Ride in a straight line. Do not weave back and forth across the road.

And every year since, I've written something in approximately the same vein, adding admonitions as they occurred to me against riding in pace lines, against drafting on vehicles, against riding like a jerk, strongly in favor of bicycle helmets, and so on. Did such admonitions help? I like to think so, but can't be cer-tain. But by 1979, I was able to write, "One of the truly encour-aging signs on RAGBRAI is the ever increasing use of bicycle hel-mets. I mean the hard ones that can save you from spending the rest of your life as a geranium." In recent years, we've had close to 100 percent of the riders wearing helmets.

When Jim Green took over from Benson in 1992 he placed an even stronger emphasis on safety, but that story must await a later chapter.

Food and drink have been a large part of the bike ride from the very first year. Then, almost everything the cyclists encountered was free of charge, and even through the last few years some things would be given away—a farmer might show up along the road on a hot day, for example, with a wagon full of watermelons that he and friends would cut up and give away on the spot.

But after that first year, there have been charges for almost all of the food and drink along the way. I'm overjoyed to report, though, that there have been almost no instances of price gouging. If anything, the opposite has been true.

Donald Kaul once wrote, "It is like being ministered to by a succession of Jewish mothers except they were Methodists and Baptists. Eat, eat, are you sure you've had enough?"

Bargains were everywhere. A Jaycees breakfast of scrambled eggs, sausage, cereal, rolls, coffee and all the milk you could drink went for $1.25 in Guthrie Center in 1974, and that was typical. A Methodist congregation in the crossroads town of Farrar made enough money selling lunch to buy a new Hammond organ for the church.

It didn't take many years for the number of food stands to increase dramatically. In the early years, I stopped at every one and took the names of those who were selling things. Later, I took the names only of nonprofit organizations—churches, fraternal organizations, lodges. Finally, a few years ago, I gave it up. My lists were becoming directories of every organization along the route.

The variety of what's offered also reflects the ethnic backgrounds of Iowa's population. When the ride went through Protivin, a mostly Czech community, the Rosary Society of the Catholic Church sold 3,000 kolaches, a marvelous pastry filled with fruit, to raise money for the church.

Amounts of food prepared were staggering even as early as the fifth year. The town of New Hampton prepared 125 pounds of ground beef, 1,000 hot dogs, 150 dozen cookies, 40 gallons of lemonade and 35 gallons of iced tea. In addition, 3,700 cupcakes were donated by the Sara Lee company from its bakeries in New Hampton.

Another example. Former *Register* reporter Robin Paley listed some of the food that people either sold or gave away on the 1978 ride. A Clinton grocer gave away slice by slice 300 watermelons, and the United Methodist Church of Washta, pop. 319, made $2,000 by selling 600 pounds of hamburgers, 400 pounds of hot dogs, 1,500 pieces of fruit and 7,500 candy bars.

As I wrote at the end of one my daily lists of food stands: "Is it any wonder that every year RAGBRAI gets fatter and fatter?"

Owners of small food establishments often became overwhelmed by the numbers of people descending on them because of the bike ride, and more than once the cyclists took over restaurants, taking orders, waiting tables, cooking on the grill.

After food and numbers of riders, the next most discussed topic, then and now, was the weather.

Sometime during the first five years it became a serious joke in our news columns, bantering that Kaul was in charge of the weather and I was in charge of the route.

On the 1977 ride a light rain fell early in the morning just as campers were about to leave New Hampton. Then a light headwind came up for most of the day. Kaul wrote:

> People began to say rude things about my powers as a weather arranger. Actually, I can explain. It was John Karras' fault. I had another nice San Diego day ready to go Wednesday night when Karras came to my motel room and said, "Your perfect weather is killing the bike trip. Bikers are reaching the campgrounds and then jogging. ... We need some lousy weather to make this trip memorable. A headwind, rain, something."
>
> "I'm sorry John," I told him. "These are lovely people and they're enjoying the ride, even if you're not. I'm going to keep giving them beautiful weather."
>
> "Kaul," Karras said, "if you won't do it for me do it for the bike trip. Giving out RAGBRAI patches for this lollipop trip is ... like getting a presidential citation from Richard Nixon."
>
> It was the Nixon crack that did it. ...
>
> "Okay, I'll see what I can do," I said. Of course you can't

do much on such short notice. I managed to get a short rain they weren't using from Minnesota, and a light easterly breeze from Nebraska. Anyway it gave the bikers something to complain about and they did seem happier. Maybe Karras is right.

But of course, there's a good reason for the weather being a hot topic when you're biking: You're out in it no matter what it's doing to you. If it rains you get wet, if the wind blows in your face you become exhausted, if it's hot and humid you sweat.

As Kaul wrote in one of his columns, "Take it from one who was there. It was a hundred and five or so. I was leaving tire marks in the concrete."

The 1979 ride gave the campers plenty of weather to talk about the night the ride stayed in Spencer. RAGBRAI almost drowned. The campgrounds at the Clay County Fairgrounds, formerly a swamp, filled up again. Some said three inches of rain fell in the night, some said six, but no matter. Lightning flashed, thunder roared and air mattresses bobbed around like corks on a pond, which is exactly what they were on. There were reports of three, four, five and six inches of water running in streams through some tents.

Buses began ferrying tenters to the Spencer YMCA, where mats were spread on floors for bedding, at about 2 a.m. The Agriculture Building on the fairgrounds was opened for others. A guitar and a banjo were produced in the Agriculture Building, and the sopping wet cyclists there joined in improvised songs to the effect that these obstacles would not slow them down. Jane Rewerts of Nevada, riding her fourth RAGBRAI, summed up the bikers' attitude early Monday when she said, "Spencer was great. The water beds were fine."

When the riders got to Rockwell City the next day they found the designated campgrounds under water. "The people in Rockwell City preparing for the riders did a lot of scrambling Monday, beginning about 2 a.m.," I reported in the next day's *Register*.

The winds had blown over several portable toilets and the plywood and canvas divisions that plumber Marv Weiss had used to transform an outdoor basketball court into a shower facility.

[Rockwell City sent tenters] to the dry areas of the fairgrounds. The elementary and junior high school grounds were open to camping. And a lot of residents were permitting campers to put up tents in their yards.

The airport was closed to planes and a caravan of recreational vehicles following the bikers, plus some tents, were put there. It's just as well the airport was closed. The runway points right at the shower facility, men on one side, women on the other—which is open to the sky.

As Benson pointed out recently, that was the start of camping in back yards, a practice that has expanded and continued to this day.

Entertainment in the evenings was another growing activity. There had been none the first year but during the second year Tracy Hardy of Muscatine brought along her bagpipes and would walk up on a hillside away from the campground in the evening and play. The campers loved the eerie sound. She said, "I love to ride my machine more than anything but playing my pipes."

On the first two rides the ending days were anticlimactic with no closing activities, but the third year Fort Madison planned a shindig for everyone. Evening entertainment during the week of RAGBRAI-III often came seemingly out of nowhere. One evening, Mike Bergman of Audubon, came out of the bike rider audience as the country fiddler and with guitarist John Corning of Cedar Falls entertained the crowd.

During the next few years there were festivities in the ending towns, often in the starting towns and often during the week.

And when there was no entertainment, the cyclists made their own. As in Mount Vernon in 1978, when the ride camped mainly on the campus of Cornell College. As I wrote at the time:

Late in the afternoon Thursday, the high school band, under some small protest from the players (or so it was said), marched their way through the campground. Riders fell in behind them, some twirling fly swatters and frame pumps in the manner of batons. The band members didn't know they were being followed until they reached the end of their course and turned around, and then cheered and were cheered by their admirers.

It was at this point, or close to it, that someone came up with the true meaning of RAGBRAI. Other things contributed to the sense of the meaning—limericks that are being chanted about RAGBRAI, songs that are being sung, things like that.

"This is not a bike ride," someone said. "It's a Scout camp for adults."

The 1977 ride from Onawa to Lansing was the easiest RAGBRAI ever. The weather was close to perfect, the days were short and the only real hills came the last two days. I heard riders complaining in Lansing, saying things like, "When is this ride going to start?"

The next year, we made sure we had a 100-mile day—Iowa Falls to Vinton—the first of many, in the route. We continued the tradition of a century day until 1986 when Benson and I finally concluded that a century was unfair to families with little kids. That's the year we started putting an optional loop in the route that would turn that day into a century ride for those who wanted one.

Most towns along the way have been quite apprehensive, even to this day, about the large group of cyclists coming to their towns. And most towns have trouble believing how clean their parks are left. "There was a scattered piece of paper here and there," said the police chief of Hawarden the first time RAG-BRAI started there, "but you can expect more trash than that from a bunch of picnickers."

That has been the story of trash for the entire life of the bike ride, and I like to think I had something to do with establishing the standard. It happened the second year in the small Benton County town of Urbana.

It was close to noon and the town was full of bikers, most of them sitting on the high curbing that lines the main street, eating lunch that they'd bought at the local grocery store and throwing their trash into the street.

The sight infuriated me. I had an entourage of four or five teen-age boys riding with me across the state that year, I never did figure out why. But I marshaled them and went to the grocery store and told the owner that I needed garbage sacks because my bike ride was trashing his town. He was so busy ringing up sales he waved me away with an "I'm too busy now."

"All right," I said, "it's your goddam town." I think I got his attention because he stopped long enough to hand me a package of garbage sacks. I distributed them to the boys and, taking one myself, we started at one end of the street and picked up trash and put it in the sacks all the way to the other. I'm pretty sure that I was muttering all the while to anyone who could hear me, "You're guests here, goddam it. Guests. You're not at home or some other dirty place."

I've never been certain that gesture did the trick, but I'm sure it made an impression. RAGBRAI has been picking up after itself ever since, especially in the campgrounds and wherever else trash barrels or dumpsters are available. It's one of my greatest points of pride to learn year after year that the campgrounds are cleaner after we leave than they were when we arrived.

Have I mentioned hospitality and acts of kindness? There were stories of kindness everywhere. A lost wallet returned by someone who had to ride five miles to catch up to the person who lost it. A purse with $65 left at a stand and when the

61

woman went back she found a note directing her to the place it was turned in. A lift to a bike shop by a woman who went out of her way to help two 18-year-olds. A 14-year-old who found two $20 bills at a food stand in a churchyard and turned them in to the lost-and-found. RAGBRAI obviously inspires a sense of community among the participants. It's like we're family, like we're all in this together, like we look out for each other. Commented Kaul, "You don't see that sort of thing going around New York City, or any place else for that matter."

As for hospitality, from the start it has fallen just short of overwhelming. And in the years from 1975–1979 it fine-tuned itself into the countryside equivalent of the Chicago Symphony Orchestra. By RAGBRAI-V and even before towns were offering free swimming, sometimes free movies, local entertainment and sometimes bands brought in from somewhere else. In Laurens there was a polka mass and a singalong. The party atmosphere was growing.

Other changes in those years were a general rise in the quality of bikes seen on the ride, a great improvement in the riding itself and a marked improvement in the general physical condition of the riders themselves.

In a 1979 pre-ride article on getting in shape, I wrote, "If past experience is any guide, 90 percent of you who show up Saturday in Rock Rapids will be in no condition to complete RAGBRAI. All you can do is hope for following winds and cool afternoons, and again, if past experience is any guide, you won't get them."

As it turned out, I was wrong. In the early years, half the riders would get off their bikes and start walking at the very sight of a hill. But on the 1979 ride, I was able to write in a story out of Humboldt: "Things are going badly on *The Register*'s Annual Great Bicycle Ride Across Iowa. People aren't complaining enough. They also aren't walking up hills the way they have in the past. ... It would be a shame but future RAGBRAIs may have to be moved to the Rockies just to get the grouching back to former levels."

One thing that didn't change, and continues to this day, were the annual rumors predicting RAGBRAI's end. In announcing the route of the 1979 ride, I wrote,

> Every year rumors crop up that this year's RAGBRAI will be the last, that *The Register* is sick of it, that Donald Kaul and I have grown bored with it, that it has become, in short, a pain in various parts of the anatomy, pick your part. One of these days all those rumors will come true and then all you mongers will be able to say you told us so. Until then, hold your tongues.

There also were many special moments and memories from those years, some good, some bad.

- The ride camped at the fairgrounds and swimming pool, opened free to the riders, in Sigourney in 1975. Unfortunately, some among our number dumped boxes of soap in the memorial fountain on the court-
house square, which outraged the local citizens. The Sigourney folks remembered that, reminded us of it and vowed they wouldn't let it happen again when RAGBRAI returned to Sigourney 20 years later in 1995.
- We also experienced our first act of vandalism in 1975 when someone spread tacks on the road out of the park in Boone. Benson and the late Bob McGehee, Boone RAGBRAI chairman that year, found themselves down on their hands and knees picking up tacks. There was a similar incident on RAGBRAI-XVII in 1989 outside of Clarinda.
- RAGBRAI-IV, in 1976, started from the rodeo grounds in Sydney in southwest Iowa. Unknown to any of us, the rodeo

63

grounds were covered with sand burrs resulting in dozens of flat tires as the cyclists tried to ride through the fields to pavement. One bike shop ran out of tubes before the ride started.

- RAGBRAI-V started in Onawa with camping on the high school grounds. The football coach had banned camping on the football field, but before anyone could do anything about it the field was covered

64

with tents. As it turned out, the tent stakes served to aerate the ground and the coach had the best crop of grass ever.

- RAGBRAI-VI in 1978, Sioux City to Clinton, is the only one Ann has missed. She took an aging aunt on a bus tour of the Pacific Northwest instead.

- Rain fell on RAGBRAI-VII between Rock Rapids and Spencer, and a construction worker in a Hartley coin laundry lent some of his clean clothes to riders to wear while they dried their soaked ones.

- That was also the year that I wrote in a story out of Fairfield, "Meanwhile, you should understand that not everyone loves RAGBRAI. Almost, but not quite. Michael Whelan of Quincy, Ill., a truck driver, is one. He took umbrage at RAGBRAI's invasion of his highway, in this case Iowa 21. His response, after he was chased down by the highway patrol, resulted in fines totaling $290 for traveling 60 in a 55 mph zone, improper passing, reckless driving and failure to yield to an emergency vehicle. It is not known if he now likes RAGBRAI any better." He had driven at least 10 miles down the wrong side of the road.

- And finally, in the same year, I was able to report that Alvino Gonzales of Dallas, Tex., and Sandra Lou Haggard, 32, of Fort Madison, were married by Judge Thomas Tucker at 6 p.m. in the RV campgrounds in Wapello. The bride and bridegroom wore cutoffs and RAGBRAI T-shirts. The guests were served hot dogs, potato salad, champagne and beer.

It was our first RAGBRAI wedding.

Sex and Drugs: Soggy Monday and a Sad Farewell, 1980–1982

Two sensational events turned the RAGBRAIs of 1980 and 1981 into especially memorable expeditions. And an announcement at the end of the ride in 1982 filled me with sorrow.

In 1980, it was a story by the then editor of *The Register*, Michael Gartner, that purported to reveal the seamy, hidden, ugly, gross underbelly of what we had been promoting for seven years as a totally wholesome, family event; a story that made the ride sound, to most who read it, like an orgy of sex and drugs.

In 1981, it was what stands out even today as the single worst day in 25 years of RAGBRAIs—a day in late July during which the temperature never got out of the low 50s, the rain never stopped and a strong wind blew in our faces. The question that day was how many riders would die of hypothermia. Amazingly, none did. We called that day Soggy Monday, and even had a patch made commemorating it.

The 1980 ride started in Glenwood and overnighted in Atlantic, Carrol, Perry, Webster City, Waverly and Elkader before ending in Guttenberg.

As Don Benson remembers it, Gartner got the idea for the sex and drugs story in Carroll from a couple of Iowa women who had ridden on many RAGBRAIs. The story showed up in *The*

Register Friday morning in Waverly. At a picnic table breakfast that morning, a middle-aged rider from Des Moines finished reading the story, wiped his mouth with a hand and muttered, "Someone else is getting my share." Another man protested, "What am I going to tell my wife?"

The general reaction from both riders and townspeople was astonishment mixed with outrage.

Ann was sitting at another picnic table with Gartner when another rider, who didn't recognize Gartner, sat down and began complaining about the story. Ann said nothing, letting Gartner hear it all. Gartner finally got up and left.

There were even suggestions that Gartner wrote the story with an eye to ending the bike ride, as in this story in the *Jefferson Herald:* "Speculation that Gartner deliberately distorted his story to give *The Register*, which sponsors the annual ride, an excuse to discontinue it does not make much sense."

Indeed, such speculation was ridiculous. I knew then and know now exactly why he wrote it. He's been a newspaperman almost from childhood, and he thought it was a legitimate story that had not been reported, so he reported it. It was as simple as that.

And it created a much greater sensation than he had counted on. The ride overnighted that day in Elkader, where the cyclists, abetted by young townspeople, mounted the rowdiest street party in RAGBRAI history. A couple of riders were pounding on Gartner's hotel door at midnight, demanding that he come out and explain himself.

Excerpts of his story follow:

WEBSTER CITY, IA. — A note was posted on the message board at the campgrounds here where 6,000 or so bicycle riders had stopped for the night. It was addressed to a girl.

"I'm sorry about the way I acted last night," it said. "I promise there will be no more animal acts. Please come to my tent." It was signed by a boy.

And that's the other side of *The Register*'s Annual Great Bicycle Ride Across Iowa.

By day, thousands of wholesome Iowans are pedaling their hearts out, downing lemonade and iced tea and homemade cookies and talking about the wonders of exercise, of Iowa and of *Register* reporters Donald Kaul and John Karras.

By night, a goodly number of these—mostly the people from 18 to 30—mass in the bars seeking just the right person to share a tent.

"If there wasn't a social side, I wouldn't be on this ride," says a 21-year-old Fort Dodge girl as she sips a beer in the trash-strewn back patio at the Seneca Street Saloon in downtown Webster City.

The "social side" is an active one. Indeed, the main thing a young man needs for this ride is not a good bicycle, insists a tan and smiling 27-year-old from Burlington.

"The chief thing you need is a good tent," he says. Pointing with pride to his $150 model, pitched in the middle of the Hamilton County Fairgrounds here. The tent, he says with pride, is equipped with "music, refreshments and good dope."

The tent, the music, the refreshments and the marijuana all but insure he will have companionship each night, he says.

Still, boy must first meet girl or, if you will, girl must first meet boy before an evening encounter can be arranged. And how do the couples meet? Some meet on the ride, some meet in the bars. ...

Somehow, the campers know which bar to hit in each town. Tuesday night, it was L'il Eva's in Perry. Wednesday night it was the Seneca Street Saloon here in Webster City. ... Kay Ross, the 22-year-old co-owner of the Seneca establishment, says her bar has been popular since it opened in Febru-

69

ary, and she figures the bikers went there because it was on the main path between the campgrounds and downtown.

Whatever the reason, the place was overflowing Wednesday night. By 9:45, some 250 people were jammed in, shouting above the deafening music, drinking beer at $2 a pitcher and making their moves. ...

Anywhere from 25 to 50 of the patrons Wednesday night were young Webster City folks to see—and perhaps to participate in—the action. "Boy, there's an awful lot of cute girls here," says a neatly bearded 26-year-old farmer as he watches the proceedings.

In all likelihood, the farmer will go home alone. Bikers tend to stick to bikers. Indeed, local girls in at least two towns met with outright rejection as they invaded the campgrounds, some bikers claim.

But once boy biker and girl biker return to the campground, anything goes. Several older campers say they have all but tripped over entwined couples seeking late-night freedom from the constraints of their tents.

The story inspired mainly outrage.

As Don Black wrote in the *Daily Gate City* in Keokuk, "RAGBRAI-VIII riders were astounded by *Register* and *Tribune* Editor Michael Gartner's account of what was happening. ... I saw thousands of bikers and gallons of lemonade but I didn't see or smell drugs or witness any sex orgies. Of course, I wasn't looking for any either."

And here is commentary in the *Mapleton Press:* "The area riders said that the spirit of RAGBRAI was dampened when *The Register* ran an article claiming that RAGBRAI was a fiasco filled with drugs and sex, and they disagree with the article, Scott Phillips, 15, said. 'There was some of that but it wasn't as bad as the article said.' Another person said, 'We were really upset about the article. It [drugs and sex] was there but you could go to the county fair and find the same thing in equal amounts.'"

Dave Yoder wrote in the Perry *Daily Chief*:

> I was shocked and amazed to hear that the thousands of bike riders that stopped in Perry July 29 were actually engaged in an orgy of drugs and sex. It came as a surprise to many of the bikers on the trip as well as to two-time veterans like myself. I don't know where Michael Gartner collected his information, but it was nowhere I had ever been on the ride.

There also were many letters to the editor in newspapers statewide expressing the same sentiments.

A day later, Donald Kaul responded in his Over-the-Coffee column:

> The guy who told you about the social scene on the RAG-BRAI campgrounds is my boss, Michael Gartner. He left the impression that practically everybody on the campgrounds is playing around with sex, smoking dope and being otherwise illicit. He didn't say that, actually, but that's the message that got through.
>
> It's a false message. There are those on the ride whose philosophy of life is considerably left of Whoopee, yes. And there are sexually active people who are ... well ... sexually active. That's true of any large gathering these days. There were sexually active people who came to Des Moines and smoked dope during the visit of the pope—take my word for it.
>
> But for the vast majority of the four or five thousand RAG-BRAI riders the week is still one of long-distance biking and lemonade. As one of the riders put it after reading Gartner's article with amazement:
>
> "How can there be so much sex with so many cold showers?" ...
>
> Bikers were incensed by his article. Loved ones left at home were outraged. Townspeople along the way were scandalized. The bikers in the campgrounds responded with bitter sar-

casm, among other things. Need any sex or drugs? a camper would yell over to the next tent. We're fine on sex but we could use a few more drugs, would come the answer. And in Elkader Friday night, a thousand or so bikers took over the streets of the town, seemingly bent on living up to Gartner's estimation of them. They climbed buildings. They mooned. They streaked. They committed vulgar acts. Had it not been for some level-headed work by some state troopers and the Elkader police, it might have turned into a really ugly scene. We'd never had a night like it before on RAGBRAI. Perhaps Gartner's piece had nothing to do with the wildness. It could be that the ride is just getting too big and the La Dolce Vita crowd is becoming larger than an essentially wholesome event can absorb.

My own view of the issue is that what you see on RAGBRAI depends largely on where you ride and where you stop. I was at the back of the pack once, on the way to Leon in 1981, and can attest that it is truly weird back there. That's where the drunks are. Also those who really belong in a hospital.

But except for that couple of hours, I've seen virtually no drunkenness and very little rowdy behavior in all the years I've been doing this ride. Of course, I don't stop in the bars, not because I disapprove of bars. I just don't like them. They're usually full of cigarette smoke and smell bad. As for sex, I know there's sex on RAGBRAI, how much I don't know, but it always has struck me that spending 8 or 10 hours crushing the pudendal nerve on an unforgiving bicycle seat is hardly conducive to passionate behavior.

The perception of the ride as a big beer binge had been catching on for several years, mainly because of the minority fringe of boozers near the back of the pack. As the ride grew in numbers so did the fringe. Gartner's piece served to reinforce that perception.

As for the rowdy street party in Elkader, here's *The Register* story about that:

> Several hundred RAGBRAIers and an indeterminate number of local youths packed a block solid with bodies for several hours. Three young men streaked nude on bicycles, two young men and a young woman mooned the crowd from the roof of a building, and so on. People cheered, drank beer and whooped it up to a fare-thee-well.
>
> Many of us grew nervous, fearing that things would get out of hand and the police would have to step in and restore order. ...
>
> What I found interesting, in rehashing the Friday night hoorah with others, was the diversity of views on how serious a threat actually existed.
>
> A *Register* reporter told me he thought a riot was imminent. Kaul and I agreed that we came close to something ugly, although I think Kaul meant violence and I meant police moving people.
>
> Another observer saw the local youths as mean and spoiling for a fight.
>
> But the crowd, or at least the RAGBRAI crowd, was never hostile, never angry, never malicious through all the hours of cheering and chanting and singing and dancing.
>
> I saw them as a bunch of little kids having a pillow fight, with the parental figures (police and other responsible adults) worrying that they were about to break the lamp.

73

The truth of the matter is that the crowd was blocking Iowa Highway 13, which at that time went right through the center of Elkader. The crowd had gathered there because of a tavern on that block, and a local state trooper was convinced that the only way to move the crowd was to wade in with billy clubs swinging. The problem was resolved when, with the help of a bull horn, members of the Team Skunk bicycle club and several state troopers, by then in plain clothes, moved the crowd around the corner onto a city street that the town had blocked off for the party.

But the 1980 ride was not totally concerned with sex, drugs and rowdy partying. Earlier in the week, RAGBRAI was treated to what was probably the most inspiring small-town reception ever.

Tiny Cooper, which almost wasn't there even in 1980 with a total population of 51, put on a show that had the cyclists shaking their heads in amazement. Terry Rich, a Cooper native, and Gerald Lawton, still a resident and then operator of the Cooper elevator, organized the reception.

Burma-Shave-style signs promoted the reception all the way from Coon Rapids to Cooper, a distance of almost 20 miles. Lawton said recently that people in the town thought the signs were stupid because there was so little to see in Cooper. The skeptics couldn't have been more wrong.

Loudspeakers had been placed in trees outside the United Methodist Church, where three food stands were located, and boomed their message at a pitch that could be heard long before the cyclists reached town.

Rich worked at an Ames radio station at the time, and recorded a continuous loop tape that mentioned the name of each of the 51 residents of Cooper.

"There are a lot of rich people in Cooper," went the line, then named all of Rich's relatives. The tape also had songs such as "Roll Out the Barrel" and "This Land Is Your Land." A small cannon was shot off periodically at the entrance to town. I remember Carter LeBeau of Davenport standing in the main street of Cooper, tears in his eyes, and shouting, "This is what America is all about."

In *Register* reporter Dave Brown's story about the day Brown quoted Steve Heer of Dubuque as saying, "This is great. It's amazing. I love it. It's spectacular. We've been waiting for miles and miles for this town." He was one of several thousand who were overwhelmed by Cooper's friendliness.

Larry Monthei, a farmer and Cooper resident, said, "This is what this country needs," indicating the thousands of bikers, all apparently enjoying themselves.

"If we had more of this, we could solve most of our problems."

The *Jefferson Herald* newspaper printed an unsigned letter that said: "Cooper is the talk of RAGBRAI. Thank you for your kind hospitality. I lost my Cooper button and would like to have another." It was one of eight letters to the editor praising the Cooper effort.

Cooper has shrunk in the intervening years. The population is down to about 35. The grain elevator is gone but part of the old elementary school—the gym and several rooms—is still there. One of the rooms houses the town's post office. The United Methodist Church is still functioning, as are Garrity's Garage and a welding shop run by Monthei. But the glorious memories of that day remain.

There were other tidbits of news in the local newspapers. An unsigned letter to the editor in the *Oakland Acorn* of Henderson reported, for example,

It was decided that the Little League Gals and the Henderson Volunteer Fire Department would try a joint venture, 'course there were those that said it was dumb and wasn't worth trying, but I really think that we proved our point. Oh, yes, it could be done and we did it. I rejoice in the feeling of cooperation that exists in our small towns and only wish there were more who could join in that comradeship of putting your shoulder to the wheel, really putting forth the effort and making it work. We knew it would be worth all the effort so a nice, tidy sum will be realized by both groups.

And there were these bits in the *Freeman Journal* of Webster City, an overnight town: "Is it always this disorganized, we asked Don Benson of *The Des Moines Register* and *Tribune.* "This is real organized," he responded with the gusto of a man who had just ridden the 67 miles (from Perry) in a car."

The day's route from Webster City to Waverly was 110 miles, one of our longer centuries, and I remember seeing Kaul coming into town walking his bike and finding his way with a flashlight.

The Waverly *Independent* reported that

> Not all the RAGBRAI travelers were totally dedicated. A group from one Iowa community confessed in a local watering hole that the ride had become much more enjoyable since they had acquired a car. They revealed that after making the first two days of the ride they tired of that mode of travel and were making the rest of the trip by car, enjoying the hospitality of the various stops without all the effort.

I can tell you even now that the ride from Elkader to Guttenberg was gorgeous. One other footnote: by 1980, we had 13 state troopers with us all week, all of them community service (or safety education) officers. They were taking turns that year riding a tandem.

Which brings us to RAGBRAI-IX, 1981, and one of the worst days of my life.

Soggy Monday aside, the 1981 route was remarkable because it was our first through southern Iowa. It had taken us that many years to find a viable route through southern Iowa. The last glaciation was to blame. Suffice it to say that southern Iowa, with its hilly terrain, doesn't have nearly the number of paved county roads as are found in the rest of the state.

And as it turned out, a stretch of gravel road in Appanoose County proved disastrous because the county engineer or the equipment operator didn't understand what Don Benson was talking about, and instead of grading the loose gravel off to the side of a road in a virtual windrow, the operator spread it evenly over a downhill run.

A lot of people fell, broke bones and went to the hospital. By the time I got to the hill someone had stationed himself at the top and was warning cyclists to get off and walk. An ambulance was at the bottom of the hill to service those who disregarded the advice.

One of the things we wanted to do in the 1981 ride was give people a good look at the beautiful Loess Hills of western Iowa. I call them Iowa's Front Range. They were formed beginning 10,000 or so years ago when the last glacier was melting and the westerly winds picked up the dust that the glacier had ground and deposited it in 200-foot hills along the east side of what is now known as the Missouri River.

So the 1981 ride started in Missouri Valley and a few miles north of the town took a county road up into the hills. A very steep county road. The problem was that a cold drizzle fell the entire first day from Missouri Valley to Mapleton, and hardly anyone looked up to see the hills. In my story of that first day, however, after writing about the bitching and moaning from the cyclists, I added:

> And yet, even in the extremes of adversity with despair as its pinnacle, these stalwart RAGBRAIers maintained a certain aplomb, if not a savoir faire.
>
> I shall carry to my grave the image of hundreds of bikers standing patiently in a steady rain outside the United Methodist Church in Pisgah waiting for the next batch of cooked hot dogs to arrive from the kitchen in the church basement. It could be a scene in a movie, but no one, save a

RAGBRAIer, would be prepared to accept such a scene as credible.

At that, I did find something good to write about Mapleton:

And Mapleton did one other thing that has been long over-due. Mapleton recognized that RAGBRAI is, indeed, a com-munity unto itself. A sign at the entrance to the campground proclaimed, "Welcome to RAGBRAI, Iowa—the only city in the state that can claim as its boundaries the Missouri River on the west and the Mississippi River on the east."

This is what Kaul wrote about that day's ride:

I don't know how to explain the first day of RAGBRAI-IX except in terms of divine retribution. It was awful. First of all, it rained ... and it was cold ... but the cold and wet could be said to have been the best things about RAGBRAI Sunday. The worst was the wind. All day long, without cease, we bucked a 20-mile-per-hour headwind ... it could have been 30. All I know is that my water bottle had white caps on it. ... there is no downside to a headwind. A headwind sucks your strength like a wolf sucks the bone marrow of a lamb.

He went on to quote Mark Twain on the guy being ridden out of town on a rail—"'If it wasn't for the honor of the occa-sion, I believe I'd just as leave walk.' That's just the way I feel about RAGBRAI. ... It isn't all sex and drugs, you know. As a matter of fact, most of the sex consists of therapeutic massage, and the drug of choice is aspirin."

That day was bad, all right, but the next day, which came to be known as Soggy Monday, was worse—incredibly worse. The temperature never rose above 52, the wind blew smartly out of the east and the rain never let up until late afternoon. For a day in Iowa in July, it was cold, bitterly cold.

As I wrote about the day:

As with all such disasters, there are many separate tales, some of which even are true. It is said, for example, that the cyclists descended on a men's clothing store in Schleswig that was holding a sale and cleaned it out. One young woman bought a man's wool suit for $5, put it on, pulled her garbage sack on over the ensemble and rode off in the rain. Three other young men bought a suit with two pairs of pants, divided the parts up among themselves and left.

A lot of people quit the ride entirely in a state of advanced demoralization ... still others left because the stress of the ride had ruined their knees or ankles.

And then quite a few people with cattle trucks and pickups turned a profit Monday by carrying drenched bikers from Schleswig to Lake City. The going rate was $5 a head.

Donald Meyer who farms near Schleswig transported bikers free. He packed his horse trailer and two other vehicles driven by his wife and daughter with bikes and bikers and refused to take a cent. "Look," he told one of the cyclists, "three weeks ago my beans and corn were an absolute disaster. The good Lord gave me this rain yesterday and today that saved my crops and the least I can do in thanks is to help out with some of these 6,000 people who've been inconvenienced by the rain that saved the whole thing that I've got invested." The people he saved kept pressing money on him and he finally agreed to take it and give it to his church.

Kaul's view was similar:

Let's be clear about one thing. The second day of RAGBRAI was not the same as the first. It was longer, it rained more and it seemed much colder. Just the headwinds were the same—brutal. My God, what a day. I mean, this isn't a bike trip, it's Moby Dick. You expect some bearded guy with a har-

79

poon to come running out of a farmyard at you yelling, "Thar She blows." ...

The reason I'm writing this from Wall Lake instead of Lake City, where the ride was scheduled to end Monday, is that I'm not at Lake City yet. I may never get there. I think I'm developing a fever. My neck hurts. My knees hurt. I want my mother.

He concluded with:

Let me say one last word about Monday.

Wretched. It was absolutely the worst day I have ever spent on a bike or off. Do you have an exercise bike? If you want to know what Monday was like, get on your exercise bike and crank down the tension so that you can hardly turn the pedals then, have someone spray you lightly with a hose while a high-speed fan blows on you. Pedal for 10 hours. That wouldn't be exactly like Monday—you wouldn't have to stand in line to go to a bathroom — but it would be close.

My story on the day's tribulations went like this:

Dear Chief:

I hope you'll excuse the sketchiness of this report on the second day of RAGBRAI. You see, there were some problems. They were the kind of problems we'll all laugh about 20 years from now, chief, but at the moment they don't seem too funny.

The day's ride, you may recall, was supposed to start in Mapleton and end in Lake City, a distance of 72 miles. For a lot of people, it ended a lot sooner. For some it ended after 20 miles. By midafternoon, trashed riders were being brought into the Lake City campground by the semi load. It was a bad day, chief.

You see, it started raining at 8 a.m. and didn't quit until

4:45 p.m. Besides that, the wind came up out of the northeast stiff enough to make strong riders wilt.

Sunday's ride dampened RAGBRAI-IX, chief, but Monday's drowned it.

As you know, chief, I've spent more than my fair share of days on a bicycle, but Monday was the most unspeakably miserable in memory. But you never know when someone's going to come along and zing you. Somewhere in the last 20 miles, just as my right hamstring was cramping and I was hoping my bike would disintegrate so I could take a ride in, I came upon this kid. Bert Steelman is his name and he's from near Lexington, Ky. He's 10 years old and about 4 feet tall, chief, and he was riding along as if the sun were out and the birds singing. Hey, I said, you're looking great. But how come you aren't on a sag wagon?

"I don't believe in sag wagons," he said. It kept me going, chief, it kept me going.

But getting back to the sketchiness of this report, you see, chief, I had problems taking notes. At first the rain made the ink run. Later, my fingers got so numb I couldn't hold the pen, and finally I wasn't seeing so good all day because my glasses were covered with water.

George Anthan of *The Register*'s Washington bureau, a RAGBRAI veteran of many years, suffered that day even more than the rest of us. His wife had suggested he take a jacket on the ride and he had replied, "Are you crazy? Who needs a jacket in Iowa in July?"

Most of the designated campground in Lake City was a sea of mud. A few camped there, but most were taken into homes. The superintendent of schools even opened up the high school gym for the cyclists even though the basketball floor had just been refinished.

The following day's story said that the day "will be remembered also for the almost frantic hospitality of the residents of

Lake City. Sodden riders were housed for the night in basements, in garages, in campers, in shelters of every description.
They were fed, showered, dried and watered. We should return
to Lake City some day in happier circumstances."

The rest of the 1981 ride was virtually without incident. In
fact, the next day the sun came out for a beautiful day from Lake
City to Greenfield. The entertainment on the Greenfield Courthouse Square was provided by the show band Festival of Skid-
more, Mo. The band was an immediate success, and appeared at
subsequent RAGBRAIs for several years.

82   Then-Gov. Robert Ray showed up early the next morning to
read a proclamation declaring Iowa the bicycling center of the
nation.

The *Greenfield Free Press* newspaper quoted Benson as saying
bikers spend $50,000 to $75,000 in each overnight town. Another newspaper, the *Centerville Iowawegian* quoted unnamed
Register officials as saying the cyclists spend $75,000 to $100,000
in each overnight town. Go figure. We know they spend a lot.

That day's ride was a 100-miler from Greenfield to Leon.
That's the day I fell behind and had to stop in Kellerton to write
my next day's story, then found myself at the back of the pack
with the drunks and the halt and lame.

The ride went through Bloomfield, and the *Bloomfield Republican* newspaper quoted Dave Kline, a member of the RAG-
BRAI medical crew at the time, as saying, "If I were a store
owner, I'd be prepared. The bicyclists really go for fresh fruit and
fruit juices, candy and other foodstuffs." He said there's a lot of
money to be made, not only in the way of retail business but for
clubs and organizations that set up stands. That kind of RAG-
BRAI advice rarely has fallen on deaf ears. The other overnight
towns were Centerville and Keosauqua before finishing in
Keokuk.

Earlier in the year, the *Times-News* newspaper of Missouri Valley quoted Benson, speaking at public meeting, as saying the

1981 ride would be the longest and hilliest ride yet. What he didn't know at the time was that it also would be the wettest.

And the sad farewell at the end of the 1982 ride? It came from my old friend and bosom cycling partner, Donald Kaul.

He wrote:

523 miles

> By any objective standard, RAGBRAI-X was a fantastic success. People kept coming up and telling me what a great time they'd had on the ride.
>
> "Did you have a good time, O.T.?" smiling faces would ask.
>
> "No," I'd say.
>
> That sort of thing has been happening the last three or four years.
>
> No more, though. I'm resigning from RAGBRAI.
>
> No tears, please. It's the end of an era, I know, but time marches on.
>
> I will miss the people; I will miss the towns. But I certainly will not miss that awful bicycle seat.
>
> I'll tell you. When I came into Keokuk Saturday, it was like V-J Day. Was it Voltaire who said: "Once, experience; twice, perversion?" What would he have said about 10 times?
>
> Perhaps the most asked question on RAGBRAI (after "Where are you from?") is, "Is there going to be a ride next year?" I don't know, but I suspect there will be. It would be dumb of *The Register* to close it down. But I will not be on it.
>
> When you think of me next year at this time, think of me elsewhere. Free at last, free at last—Great God Almighty, I'm free at last.

83

And except for a few times since that he's returned for RAGBRAI as a guest, he's kept his word.

RAGBRAI Matures, 1983–1985

By 1983, most of the changes that were shaping RAGBRAI as we know it today either were developing or were already in place. That is, the planning and organization process had become very sophisticated, the multitude of bike clubs and teams that go on the ride had organized or were organizing by then, and communities in Iowa knew what RAGBRAI was all about. Many had started asking us to bring the ride to them. (In the early years Benson and I would spend hours with Chamber of Commerce persons telling them what was about to happen to their communities, and they refused to believe us until the event actually happened. Then they'd say, in effect, "I don't believe it.")

Which doesn't mean everything was going smoothly. Hardly. There were three major changes in the years 1983–85 and a big shock.

The first change came in 1983, when we began charging a RAGBRAI fee.

The second also happened in 1983 when Donald Kaul, my old friend and co-founder of RAGBRAI, made good on his promise of the previous year to resign from the bike ride, and Chuck Offenburger, author of the Iowa Boy column, joined me as co-host.

The shock came in 1984, RAGBRAI-XII, with the first deaths in the history of the event.

The third change hit in 1985, when Lois Peterson, then the office manager for RAGBRAI, sent RAGBRAI credentials to everyone who asked for them. (The way the decision actually was made is lost in the mists of time. Lois says there's no doubt that Don Benson, the RAGBRAI coordinator, was involved in the decision. She didn't do it on her own, she said. She recalled that they figured they wound up giving everyone tags anyway because of cancellations, so decided to just send them out to everyone that year. Benson doesn't remember it that way, but no matter.)

They were yeasty years.

The RAGBRAI fee decision came about this way. *The Register* lost money for the first time in its history in one of the quarters in 1982, and then-publisher Gary Gerlach decreed that all future *Register* promotions would have to pay their own way.

We RAGBRAI organizers anguished over that order for a long time, discussing all manner of ways to comply. Fortunately, most of the ideas, such as selling RAGBRAI to an Iowa corporation, arrived stillborn, and we finally settled on a rider fee.

The first year's fee was $12.50, and the point was simply to recover expenses. Incidentally, in the early years *The Register* was able to mount the bike ride for under $10,000 a year. Today, the budget is more than $300,000 a year, including money that is returned to the host communities.

From the start, management determined that any RAGBRAI funds left over after expenses would be donated to non-profit or charitable organizations, and that policy has continued under Gannett ownership.

The second big change came with the departure of Kaul from RAGBRAI and the arrival of Offenburger. Chuck has a great story about how he got into RAGBRAI, and I'll let him tell it in his own words.

87

It was 1983 and Don Kaul, two weeks before RAGBRAI, called Jim Gannon, the editor of *The Register,* and told him he decided he was not going to go on RAGBRAI eleven.

So Gannon called me into his office and told me this, and said that he felt that they really wanted two folks from the newsroom out there to write the RAGBRAI stories.

So he said do you want to go with Karras and I said, well, I guess I would if it was okay with Karras and he'd already talked to Karras and said that that'd be okay.

So I said what do I do about a bicycle? Do I go out to Sears or something? He said you just get in touch with John and he'll get you all set up. So I called Karras and he sent me to Forrest Ridgway out at Bike World to get equipped with a bike, and Forrest asked me some questions about myself.

I remember telling him that I was an old baseball catcher and I had either one or two knees that were a little shaky. So Forrest said he was going to get me on a bike with especially low gears and he got me this 18-speed Trek, which I'm still riding.

I got that bicycle the day I was leaving Des Moines with my two young kids and heading up to South Dakota, Mount Rushmore and the Black Hills on a vacation of four or five days. So I took my bike and the kids' bikes up to South Dakota and that's where I did my first few rides, none of which were more than a couple of miles or maybe three miles.

I got back to Des Moines and I knew I wanted to try to get into shape ... I'm down now to about a week before that first RAGBRAI, and I knew I needed to get a little more mileage in. So I got done at work one day about 2 in the afternoon and headed home and thought, aha, I've got enough time here to get out and get a good bike ride in.

I pulled on a pair of gym shorts, no shirt, and tennis shoes and took off from my house, which is in northwest Des Moines, and rode out through Johnston, going okay, and decided maybe I could go for Grimes. So I pedaled on out Highway 44 to Grimes, and got there and was still feeling good, rode through Grimes and decided, oh, I'm going for Dallas Center.

So I headed out west of Grimes and got out there somewhere and all of a sudden it occurred to me that I was starting to get thirsty. I had no water bottle with me, I didn't know you were supposed to do that, and I was going to have to ride all the way back, and I thought, well, I better turn around. But instead of turning around I decided to head south and come back in a different way.

So I headed south down toward the Waukee area. I remember starting to really get in trouble being thirsty, and stopped at a farm to see if I could get a drink of water. No one was home and there was no farm pump outside to get a drink so I headed on in and rode all the way back to the west side of Des Moines where I ran into a Quick Shop or Quik Trip out on Hickman Road.

By the time I got there I was in real trouble. I was seeing pretty colors, I think maybe I'd stopped sweating and I probably was totally dehydrated. So I walked right into that store, went right to the cooler in the back and grabbed a big jug of

Gatorade and sat down on the floor right there in the store and started drinking it.

I was just gasping back there, I was so shot. I finally became aware that somebody was standing there near me and I looked up and the store manager said, "Mister are you in trouble here?" and I said, well, I know this looks terrible but I said I think I'm all right. If I just sit here and finish this Gatorade, I think I'm going to be okay.

So I did that and I got up and back up to the front of the store and he was there at the checkout counter and that's when it occurred to me I had not brought my billfold. I had no money. And so, embarrassed as hell, I introduced myself to him and told him I was trying to get ready for RAGBRAI, and I would go home and get my wallet and come right back out and pay him for the Gatorade, which I did and he let me do that.

So I rode the next three probably four miles home, I made it home, it had been about 30 miles, my longest bike ride ever.

I called the Karrases to check in with John. He wasn't home and Ann asked if I wanted to leave a message, I said this is Offenburger and you just tell him I want to kill the son-of-a-bitch.

But I took off from there, somehow made it through that first RAGBRAI, I went into it with no more than 50 or 60 total miles. It's been a real learning experience ever since and it's been a great time, but kind of a rough start for me.

Offenburger's story on RAGBRAI-XI after the first day's ride of 62 miles, twice as far as he'd ever ridden a bike before, went like this:

I made it all the way into Harlan without walking up a single hill. Then I ate dinner, went to bed and waited for the leg cramps to come. Not a one. Monday morning there was no pain and only a little stiffness. ... I think I owe it all to the guy I met in the restroom line at Tater's Pub in Dunlap about noon. ... "What you have to do," said this wise man whose name I neglected to get, "is avoid electrolytic imbalance." (These bikers often talk a different language, I've discovered, especially when they are discussing either body chemistry or the gear-shift mechanism.)

"OK, avoid electrolytic imbalance," I said. "How do I do that?"

"Bananas and beer," he answered.

Thereafter, I'm sure I established a new one-day personal record for banana consumption, and, yes, I made it to most of the beer stands, too. I took good care of my electrolytes, and my electrolytes, it turned out, took good care of me.

Offenburger also found the true meaning of RAGBRAI his first year on the ride. He found it in the experience of Bill Johnson, 27, of West Palm Beach, Fla., who cycled in intense pain into the town of Dows looking for relief.

His legs "were rubbery," Offenburger wrote, "from the strain of riding the western Iowa hills earlier in the week. His ankles were swollen. He was about whipped mentally, too."

Johnson walked into Larsen Clothing and asked Clifford Larsen where he could rent a room. He wanted to soak his feet. There are no motels in Dows, Larsen told him, but he'd call a woman who often rents rooms. No answer. So Larsen called his wife, Gladys, whom everyone knew as Gladdie, and asked if the rider could drop over. Sure, she said.

Johnson found his way to the Larsen home and Gladdie was there to meet him. She offered him a shower, which he gladly accepted, then threw his dirty clothes in the washer and gave him some of Clifford's things to put on while his were washing and drying.

The visitor showered, used Cliff's razor, wore Cliff's shorts and came out to the living room where Gladdie poured water in a bucket for his feet. She positioned a fan so it would blow more cool air on him and fixed him a brunch of bacon and eggs. All the while, they chatted.

Two hours later, the refreshed Johnson was ready to return to the road.

"I asked her how much money I could pay her," he said. "She said she wouldn't think of taking any money. I didn't push the point because I could tell she was so genuine in not wanting money that it would've been wrong for me to insist."

Offenburger concluded the story this way:

> Now, after I heard about this, I tried out the story on a few of my new friends as we were pedaling toward Dubuque.
>
> The Rev. Art Seaman, a minister in Shelby in western Iowa, made me realize what the best part of the story is. "That kind of thing," he said, "happens over and over, year after year, on this ride."
>
> It is what RAGBRAI is really all about.
>
> I feel good to be a part of it.

In a prophetic aside in a story a couple of weeks before RAGBRAI-XI began I had written: "This will be Offenburger's first experience of RAGBRAI. May he find the roads smooth and the winds favorable. He plans to ride a bicycle at least part of the way, and might even discover what so many of us discovered years ago, that cycling can become addictive."

And how. Not only did he find it addictive, he's become even more of a cycling nut than I, going as far as to lead a ride 5,000 miles across the United States in 1995 as a prelude to the Iowa sesquicentennial celebration the next year.

Then, in the middle of the week of RAGBRAI-XI in 1983, I wrote the following out of Clarion, Iowa:

> Daily, people on *The Register*'s Annual Great Bicycle Ride Across Iowa-XI and folks along the road ask me if I miss Donald Kaul.
>
> "Where's your buddy?" they say.
>
> "Do you think Kaul will show up the last day?" they say.
>
> "Who are you going to make fun of without Kaul here?" they say.
>
> Good question, that last one. How could anyone make fun of anyone who calls himself Iowa Boy? And especially when that Iowa Boy is a guy like Chuck Offenburger.
>
> I must admit I had some misgivings about hearing that they were sending Offenburger in for Kaul after Kaul announced for the 500th and final time that he was all RAGBRAIed out.
>
> Oh, I had no doubt that Offenburger would do a good job. Nor was I concerned that their writing styles and outlooks on life are 20 degrees apart. No, my doubts dealt more with the show-biz aspects of RAGBRAI.
>
> After all, Kaul and I have been doing this routine in the center ring for 10 years. You don't break up a team like that and send just anyone in as a replacement.
>
> For 10 years, we were the Abbott and Costello, the Burns and Allen, the Bob and Ray, the Frick and Frack of Iowa bicycling. Kaul and Karras meant RAGBRAI to a whole generation of Iowa bicyclists. Offenburger and Karras? Karras and Offenburger? I wondered.
>
> But now, halfway through the week, all doubts and fears have been allayed. Sending Iowa Boy in for Kaul has worked out beautifully for me. Indeed, there's been hardly any change.
>
> Kaul rode slow. Offenburger rides slow (the Iowa Boy did beat me into town Wednesday, something Kaul never did on

a bike, but I mark that down as a once-off aberration, as the product of excess Boyish enthusiasm brought on by a 25-mile-an-hour tailwind).

I didn't see Kaul from one day to the next, and I rarely see Offenburger from one day to the next. People used to ask me, "Where's Kaul? At the back of the pack?" Now they ask me, "Where's Offenburger? At the back of the pack?"

About the only real change is that it takes me longer to type Offenburger than it did to type Kaul. I can live with that.

And after the ride was over, in a retrospective column, Offen-   93
burger ended a story about a young man whose mother deplored his living from RAGBRAI to RAGBRAI with this comment:

> When I think about what his mother said, even though I am just a RAGBRAI rookie, and one of a more advanced age, I nevertheless rather resemble that remark.
>
> I want to do it again.
>
> But I have an awful thought. Let's just say I remain on board as a host, co-host or whatever I was of this thing until I am the same age that John Karras was this summer. Do you realize we'd be out there on RAGBRAI-XXVIII?

There were other notable differences in 1983's ride. For example, we were attended at one overnight stay by the ride's first (I think) massage therapist. As I noted in a July 3 RAG-BRAI story, "Mary Dengler, a registered mas-sage therapist, will have a massage booth set up in Ames for those with aching muscles. The charge will be $5, and no snickering, please. She offers only the legitimate kind of massage. No green doors here." The first masseuse on RAGBRAI? Probably.

We also returned to Guthrie Center, scene of our great success in 1974, for an overnight stay in 1983. Dean Osen, the truck driver, was still there and we recapped our arm-wrestling match of nine years earlier, when I said he had let me win and he said I cheated. As I wrote in the July 27, 1983, *Register,* "We battled to a draw twice, although I don't think Osen was really trying. As I strained to put his hand down, he would reach over with his free hand to take sips of beer from a plastic cup. This time, I think he let me draw."

The next year, 1984, the ride started in Shenandoah, Offenburger's home town, in honor of his joining the ride as co-host. We couldn't begin there in 1983 because he joined the ride almost at the last minute, after the route had been set.

The week started out very hot and very hilly, but the two deaths that year stunned us. We had gone through 11 RAG-BRAIs without one, and probably had been lulled into thinking that we never would have any.

The first death occurred early in the week when Mark Alfred Knief, 28, of Oelwein collapsed at the top of a steep hill west of Corning and died of a heart attack. The temperature that day reached 100 degrees. It was learned later that he had a damaged heart.

RAGBRAI coordinator Don Benson was quoted in the next day's *Register* as saying, "We have felt for years that we've been very, very fortunate about this. It's not only fortunate but unusual that you could have what really amounts to a town of 7,000 or more people, all of them on two wheels, without having some of the normal things that happen in any community that size— including, of course, deaths. We've been lucky."

Later in the week, Janet Newell, 30, a registered nurse then of California and formerly of Davenport and Iowa City, disappeared in Ottumwa and later was found drowned in the Des Moines River. Friends reported that she had been feeling ill, but the death remains a mystery to this day.

But not all of the 1984 ride was death and solemnity.

Riders were treated, for example, to a performance by the Granny Squad of Hedrick in south-central Iowa. The women, all of whom had granddaughters on the Hedrick girls' basketball team, formed their group in the fall of 1983 when no one turned out for the school's cheerleading squad. They were gathered at Hedrick's food stand along the road in 1984 between Ottumwa and Mount Pleasant.

And after much urging, they performed one of their cheers: "Let's get fired up," clap, clap, clap-clap-clap, "Let's get fired up," clap, clap, clap-clap-clap. There was no dancing, no leap- 95 ing, no fancy formations, but they more than made up in enthusiasm what they lacked in athleticism.

The main feature of the next year's ride in 1985, of course, was the astoundingly large horde of cyclists that rode out of Hawarden on the way to Clinton. Benson was quoted as saying that that was the first year any applicants for the ride had to be turned away, but methinks he dissembled because he later said that everyone who applied got tags, and there had to be at least 10,000 cyclists on the road out of Hawarden.

And with that number, we finally got the answer to a question that had been haunting us from the start: What happens if this ride gets too big?

We'd imagined all sorts of things—towns running out of food, water, toilet paper, patience—but had never even considered the real answer, which was: There was hardly any room on the road to ride. It was wheel to wheel for the first three days. By Tuesday, I wanted to go home, but by the end of that day the cyclists, displaying more wisdom than all of the RAGBRAI managers could put together, had spread out on the road and relaxed.

Other features of RAGBRAI-XIII in 1985:

- The money we returned to the host towns after the ride reached $3,000 each that year, much to each community's surprise. We kept the practice of returning funds secret for many years, and it was always fun to see the shock and pleasure when the envelopes were opened, especially in the smaller overnight towns, where a few thousand dollars meant a lot.

- Offenburger and I played against two Iowa high school girls' basketball stars that same year. Both of them clobbered us. We played two-on-two against Lynne Lorenzen and a teammate in Ventura, and against Molly Tideback and a friend in Waterloo. Both went on to fine college careers.

  Offenburger set up the challenges, as he did in several subsequent years. It took me several years to come to my senses and just say no to such nonsense.

- There was another fatality. Charles Kithcart, 40, of North Liberty, died in Emmetsburg when a woman lost control of a van and it jumped the curb and ran over Kithcart, who was walking his bicycle along the sidewalk at the time.

  There has been a total of 15 deaths during RAGBRAIs through 1997, and another in connection with an accident that happened on RAGBRAI two years earlier. Only one, however, was directly related to cycling. That happened in 1987 when John Boyle, 19, of Rockwell City fell under the wheels of a flatbed trailer carrying a fiberglass swimming pool.

  The others who died and the causes of death were Ramani Ramachandran, 29, of Madras, India, a University of Iowa doctoral candidate, drowned in a farm pond in 1986; Allen Gene Polikowski, 45, of Denison, heart attack in 1989; Thomas Short, 26, of Wheaton, Ill., broken neck in a mudsliding accident, died two years later; Darrell Fox, 46, of Council Bluffs, heart attack in 1991; Jon Dominick, 31, of Iowa City, found dead at his campsite in 1993, history of allergies and asthma; Shirley Mae Cottrell, 50, of Dubuque, and her mother-in-law, June Cottrell, in her 70s, killed when their van was struck by a truck in 1993; Madeleo Blake, 81, of Letts, heart attack in 1995; Charles W. Lackmann, 55, of Mason City and Norman Dietrich, 60, of Ames, heart attacks, and Kurt Schukhart, 25, of Cedar Falls of a rare blood vessel disease, all in 1996; and LeRoy Curry, 61, of Windsor Locks, Conn., heart attack in 1997.

- The ride that year also was accompanied daily by two antique double-wing airplanes. Gary Lust of Iowa City and Linley Wright of Glen Rose, Tex., a retired pilot, who met at an antique airplane show, both flew British-built DeHaviland Tiger Moths along the route. Lust's wife Sharon, son Karl and daughter Amy were on the bike ride. Wright's wife, Martha, with granddaughter, Jana, drove a motor home from airport to airport.

    I was offered a ride in the plane but dislike flying and was happy to have Ann substitute for me. She found it great to see all the tents clustered in Humboldt. Another time she went up on a two-seater ultralight plane over the Missouri River flood plain. Ann likes to get high.

- We also had another 83-year-old along. Henry Braafhart, 83, was riding with his wife Leona, 63, of Orange City.

- The ride has had national and international coverage, beginning with a story about 1974's second ride in *Sports Illustrated*. Stories about RAGBRAI have appeared in every major newspaper and in many magazines in the United States and abroad. Each one has brought a new spate of inquiries. Along in 1985 were reporters from the *Orlando Sentinel, Rocky Mountain News* of Denver, *Chicago Sun-Times, San Francisco Chronicle, National Geographic Traveler, St. Paul Pioneer-Press, San Diego Union* and several Iowa radio and TV stations.

- That also was the first year of increased medical and safety staffs. A fourth ambulance was added with two additional medical technicians, bringing the total to eight. Three more Iowa State Troopers were assigned to traffic control, bringing

97

the number of those accompanying the ride all the way across the state to nine. In the past, six troopers, wound up working incredibly long shifts.

- In addition to having the largest number of riders up to that year, 1985's route was the longest RAGBRAI ever at 540 total miles.

The Fine-tuning Years,
1986–1997 In the years from 1986 to the

present, the changes in RAGBRAI have amounted more to

adjusting and correcting rather than dealing with wrenching

and unforeseen problems. Not that each year's ride is totally

predictable or easy to manage.

If anything, organizing and managing RAGBRAI has become more complicated and more difficult than ever. Everything connected to the event has expanded, from the numbers of clubs, teams and riders to the array of RAGBRAI merchandise *The Register* now offers and the revenue the ride generates. What began as a modest lark has turned into an industry.

The major changes since 1985 have involved a big change in management when Don Benson, RAGBRAI coordinator since the beginning in 1973, retired after 1991's ride, and the development of several new programs and practices by his successor, Jim Green.

(Early on, I nicknamed Benson the wagonmaster, in keeping with RAGBRAI's evoking images of the famed cattle drives of the Old West. I tried to hang the title of trail boss on Green, but he objected. Not only did Green dislike the name, so did almost all of the regular RAGBRAI riders responding to a poll, so I retreated. He's just RAGBRAI coordinator.)

There also have been many creative and imaginative entertain-

Don Benson (left) *and Chuck Offenburger pondering a route*
Ann Karras Photo

ments and events put on by communities along the way over the years. It seems like every time we conclude we've seen it all, some town surprises us with something different.

Benson worked in what used to be called *The Register* and *Tribune*'s promotion department (now marketing services, but what's in a name?) his entire career at the paper, from 1958 until he took early retirement in 1985. His various assignments included working with circulation promotion (hired because of his news background) and expanded into classified promotion. He was educational services director off and on; got more involved in public events, became public events manager; then public relations director; all the time, contining to work with advertising, circulation and news departments.

He was associated with RAGBRAI from the start, before it was called RAGBRAI, and provided distinguished and imaginative leadership and counsel throughout his association with the ride. He also developed the practices we still use today, with modifications, in mapping each year's route in December and driving it in February. Then meeting regularly with the host communities to assist them in the difficult and complex planning and public relations efforts that are required if the ride's visit is to be a success.

Jim Green spent 23 years, starting at age 28, working in *The Register* and *Tribune*'s circulation department, where his assignments included district manager, assistant zone manager, morning manager for Des Moines, manager of the service center and telemarketing, and finally circulation sales manager.

He applied for and got the RAGBRAI job after Benson announced 1991 would be his last year. RAGBRAI had always been a part-time job for Benson, both while he was in the Promotion Department and after he took early retirement in 1985. When Green took over in 1992 it was as a full-time assignment, with only a couple of other much smaller projects included in his duties.

Here is Green's account of how he got involved in RAGBRAI in 1983, cycling with Offenburger as friend and helper:

> Chuck and I started at the same time, same year. Don Benson and I were very close and he kept gnawing at me that I couldn't do it and that I was a wuss, and so forth. And I was going to show him. But the bottom line is he probably was very much right because I remember coming home after that ride and thinking God had forsaken me and I was gonna die and Judy [his wife] said,
>
> "You're hooked aren't you," and I said you bet I am but I'll be in better condition next time.
>
> In those early years I still worked in the Circulation Department, and I got carriers and district managers involved in this great event for the first time. I would go out with Don once in the spring to every town and I'd hold carrier meetings

and we'd sell these subscriptions and these coffee cups and try to up the circulation as much as we could and build up enthusiasm not only in the communities we were going through but also into the carrier organization. The biggest number we had on any given day was 100 carriers riding with me. We've had 60-some ride the whole week with me.

One of my responsibilities besides the carriers was to kind of make sure that Chuck got along. I enjoyed meeting all the people because he met the characters, the good people, the bad people on RAGBRAI and it gave me a completely different perspective. At the same time my challenge was to make sure that he got in by 4 o'clock so that he could write.

I had a great advantage over Benson in that for eight years I got to enjoy what a great ride this was, seeing it from a bicycle seat, and he never did.

And then on RAGBRAI-XIX I applied for and got this job. It's like I died and went to heaven. It's the greatest thing that I've ever done. For one year I trained under Benson, and this gentleman taught me more in one year than I probably learned in the other 40 or 45 that I was alive. How to deal with people, how to work with people, how to convince them that it was their idea. Benson did a phenomenal job of training.

The biggest challenge came in RAGBRAI-XX when we had a meeting with the Iowa State Patrol and the Department of Transportation, and I was flat-out told that I had one year to get the safety on RAGBRAI turned around or they couldn't be a part of it. That was because coming out of Atlantic on RAGBRAI-XIX we took up all four lanes of the highway for part of the day.

Tim Lane and I, driving home from Mason City one night in 1992, came up with the idea of *Ride Right*, which is probably one of our greatest accomplishments. The goal is promoting safety through positive reinforcement.

The state patrol's biggest concern now is our numbers. We have to work on that and continue to keep them under control so that we can keep the numbers at about 10,000, because that's fair to the people along the route. Some of our greatest successes are in safety. We've had years of 98 percent helmet usage, which is tremendous.

Benson did a phenomenal job of setting the foundation of this super ride, and all I have done is carry on in the tradition, or tried to, in the tradition he set up.

Green has done a stellar job. He took the traditions that Benson left and honed them, polished them, expanded them and fine-tuned them into an even smoother operation. He also has initiated several projects in conjunction with RAGBRAI, the most successful of which is the bike safety campaign called Ride Right.

RAGBRAI had emphasized bicycle safety for years, and the purpose of the new campaign was to focus even more attention on the subject. The main thrust was to get the old and established Iowa bicycle clubs involved in safety campaigns. Ride Right chairs were named throughout the state and charged with getting their communities, and especially the schools, talking about bicycle safety. Each year, the RAGBRAI community that displays the most compelling and imaginative safety displays is named that year's winner of the Ride Right safety contest.

The campaign has been a marked success, and has been adopted by 191 clubs and organizations in 42 states, by 43 commercial tour operators and 170 community clubs or organizations. In addition, the Iowa State Patrol uses Ride Right materials in safety presentations at schools throughout the state, and 32 local law enforcement programs use the materials in bicycle rodeos and other safety promotions.

Other projects started by Green were a contest by schools in host towns for the best decoration of the cardboard appliance boxes used as trash containers at RAGBRAI campgrounds; and another contest in which school classes design and put together a promotion campaign for a theoretical RAGBRAI route. Some of the entries have approached professional quality with sophisticated audio-visual presentations and even web pages.

Green's most recent project was the formation of what he called the *Dream Team,* a group of inner-city Des Moines youngsters who were recruited through the Des Moines YMCA, outfitted with bicycles and sent along, with adult companions, to ride RAGBRAI. The first group joined the 1997 ride, the twenty-fifth. The project has continued since.

But what was probably Green's most significant innovation was his decision to return to the host communities to check on their planning progress and problems (or "challenges," as he insists on calling them) on a regular schedule from the middle of February to the middle of July, almost to the day the ride begins. Green visits the host communities in the west half of the state on Monday, Tuesday and Wednesday of one week and those in the east half the same days of the next.

When he first started that in 1992 I thought it an unnecessary commitment of time, but the value became obvious on a return visit to Keokuk, that year's ending town, to meet with the town's RAGBRAI committee in the fall.

One of the committee members said, "We got kind of tired of seeing Green, but we knew he was going to be here every other Monday so we figured we'd better have some progress to show him." And it soon became obvious that his regular visits were paying big dividends, because the host communities never had been better organized and prepared for the cyclist invasion.

Benson also had checked in regularly with the host communities, but on a more casual basis than Green's rigid schedule. Green simply took Benson's operation one more step.

One corollary of RAGBRAI over the years has been a proliferation of multi-day bike rides in states across the country, almost all of them spin-offs from the experience of RAGBRAI. This started early on, with cross-state rides in Florida, Nebraska, Oklahoma, Colorado and Michigan being among the earliest.

The rides became so numerous that the coordinators in 1990 finally formed an organization, the National Bicycle Tour Directors Association, with Benson as the first director. In fact, he was one of the instigators. The group meets annually to exchange ideas and solutions to various problems. It now has 43 members representing 43 rides, with more on the way. Naturally, Jim Green is a member, and was director in 1993–94.

One thing has not changed in all these years: the annual February scouting trip. It is just as brutal as ever, perhaps more so. The first year, of course, we didn't do much of anything ahead of time, but beginning with SAGBRAI, we drove the route in late winter. Benson, Kaul, Ann and I were along for certain. I don't think there was anyone else. Later, Benson and I were joined by Trooper Bill Zenor on those trips.

What they amounted to, in short, was four or five 10- to 14-hour days in the company van. Benson always drove, sometimes maddeningly. Typically, he would drive into one of our designated host communities and commence driving around and around, wordlessly, seemingly aimlessly.

Finally, unable to stand it any longer, I'd say, "What are you looking for, Don?"

And he'd bark back, "Relax, Johnny. Just relax," and never tell me what he was looking at or for.

It was great sport, believe me.

Jim Green has continued the tradition, with variations. Like Benson, he does all the driving but unlike Benson is willing to communicate. He also runs an occasional stop sign, which Benson never did, and has been known (even with a state trooper in the van) to back up a hill on a two-lane country road after missing a turn.

I wrote a column about scouting the route that appeared in

the Feb. 13, 1983, *Sunday Register*. That was a long time ago, true, but it is just as valid today as it was then.

I am writing this in a motel room in Harlan on a Monday night. I do not want to be in Harlan on Monday night. I have nothing against Harlan, understand. It is just one of 10,000 places I don't want to be on a Monday night. Where I want to be on a Monday night is home.

I wanted to be home watching public television. I can't even remember what it was I wanted to watch on public television. I think it was "Mystery!" which at this time is doing a series of Sergeant Cribb stories. I missed "Mystery!" and whatever else there was to see and ate dinner at the Evergreen Inn instead.

Ah, but I digress.

We are, the three of us—Don Benson, *The Register*'s director of public relations, William Zenor of the Iowa State Patrol, and I—in this week, as we have in 10 previous years in the month of February, scouting the route of yet another *Register*'s Annual Great Bicycle Ride Across Iowa.

Here is how the week goes.

We begin the week in high spirits but in low expectations. Remember, we have done this many times before, and know that by Wednesday night, wherever that happens to be, we will be at each others' throats.

Zenor and I refer to Benson as "the mad driver," because he never wants to stop. He doesn't want to stop for breakfast. He doesn't want to stop for lunch. He doesn't want to stop to let anyone go to the bathroom. The only thing he wants to stop for is gas. When he stops for gas, the rest of us grab all the gusto we can before we have to get back into the company van.

As we drive, which is what this week is all about—driving—we look at maps. We look at state maps. We look at county maps. We look at traffic count maps. And we try to calculate how many broken clavicles will lie between the beginning and the end of the ride if we take this road or that. We try to project the number of blown knees and spavined hips if we take 70 rather than 50 miles of hills in one day's ride.

This is a no-win situation, friends, a no-win situation. On the other hand, it is a no-lose situation. I can always say that this is my ride and as such it will go where I want it to go, as far as I want it to suffer, and any idiot who accompanies me in such frivolous enterprise deserves whatever he gets.

Ah, yes. So I can't lose. Except that deep down in my heart of hearts (and even deep down in Donald Kaul's heart of hearts, if he has a heart of hearts), I know that what I really want is that people who attend RAGBRAI have a good time. That is what Kaul and I have had in mind from the start—and Benson, too, and even Zenor if he were pressed on it. All of us want everyone who participates in RAGBRAI to have a good time. That's what it's all about, after all—having a good time.

So Benson and Zenor and I set out across the state. We drive—Benson drives—the company van to the western terminus of the route. Then we work our way back to the center of the state, stopping in the overnight stops, talking to the Chamber of Commerce folks, telling them that RAGBRAI will be arriving on whatever date, and that they should lock up whatever virgins they can find in the town (Ha! and again, Ha!), and that they really won't have to rebuild.

But the tale grows tedious. Suffice it to say that in this week on the road, this interminable week on the road, we drive across the state twice, that we cover the RAGBRAI route backward and forward, that we hone it, we refine it, we cozen it, we polish it, we shine it until we can't stand it and each other for most of another year.

All I can say is that I hope all of you have as much fun on RAGBRAI-XI as I intend to have. It's my route, you know.

You poor turkeys, you.

Here are highlights of the RAGBRAIs themselves from 1986 through 1997:

RAGBRAI-XIV, 1986

This was the first year we put an optional century loop in the route, which went from Council Bluffs to Muscatine with overnights in Red Oak, Audubon, Perry, Eldora, Belle Plaine and Washington. Benson and I finally had decided that a natural 100-mile day was unfair to families with young children, and settled on the optional loop as the way of satisfying the machismo riders who wanted to say they'd done a century.

Not only did we have our first optional loop that year (between Perry and Eldora) but at least one young woman rode the loop twice by mistake. Brenda Johanson, then 17, of Des Moines missed the turn at the end of the loop and went around twice. I found her weeping uncontrollably and afraid that her entire family would laugh at her and she would miss her dinner. I saw her the next day and everything had turned out just fine.

Incidentally, the loop is the same one we did in 1998 between Boone and Eldora.

Also in 1986, the city of Washington, Ia., playing off its town motto of the "Cleanest City in Iowa," guaranteed that everyone who wanted one would have a hot shower.

Arizona Gov. Bruce Babbitt, an announced candidate for the Democratic nomination for president, was along with his family that year, all cycling the entire way. Babbitt's attendance produced a hilarious evening in Red Oak the first night of the ride. A Red Oak family threw a party honoring Trooper Bill Zenor's role in Red Oak. Unknown to those of us at that party, a reception was being held for Babbitt in the yard next door, shielded by a high wooden fence between the yards.

Every time those of us at the Zenor party applauded a tribute to Zenor, louder applause, even shouting, would come roaring back from the other side of the fence. I learned later that those at the Babbitt reception thought a Republican rally was being held next door, and every time we cheered, they were urged to cheer louder and show those Republicans where America's true political preferences lay.

RAGBRAI-XV, 1987

I sat this one out with a heart attack, but Ann took over my role of co-host for the week and went to all the receptions, made the short speeches and participated in all the rest of the events that I usually attend.

109

This is what she remembers about that year:

I felt very sad that John was unable to join us. I knew he was just desolate but he encouraged, begged me to go for him while our son came out and stayed with his dad. I went. It was an interesting experience to stand on the stage for the welcoming even though I said very few words, something to the effect of how John was doing well and wished he could be here. Near the last day when I got a second chance to speak my words in reference to an early-morning storm were, "This must be John's revenge for not getting to go on the ride."

I vaguely remember the town of Little Turkey and sandwiches (always remember food) but I don't remember the song "Turkey Day," possibly because it was unmemorable. Yes, I did see the church at St. Lucas but did not ride my bike up that hill. There were enough other hills in the area to more than satisfy my craving for riding hills. My desire for hills is a high minus figure. In fact, I have never taken a hill I could avoid.

John joined us at West Union, but not on his bike. We went together to the courthouse square where the town put on one of the biggest party nights ever—a different band at each corner of the square. It was a jumble of flashing lights loud music, and huge crowds who just loved it.

This was the year the bikers helped find a child lost in a cornfield. The search ended successfully when the child emerged at the other side of the field.

This also was the first RAGBRAI for Ben Davidson, retired Oakland Raiders all-pro defensive end and a one-time actor in Miller Lite television commercials. He told John he had "heard about RAGBRAI when I was in Iowa for a charity telethon, and I decided right then I'd see if I could go. Since I've quit playing football, I've done a lot of bicycling, and I wanted to give this a try." At 6 feet 8 inches with his trademark handlebar mustache, Davidson is an imposing figure, on a bike or off. He has ridden many RAGBRAIs since.

I believe this also was the year I had dinner with Davidson. Ben said that on RAGBRAI he probably gained a lot of weight. When I looked at the dinner he ate I was not surprised. My friend Carolyn Lynner was with me and neither of us knew or cared anything about football. Davidson's charm and humor about our ignorance made the dinner more memorable than ever.

I never got to University of Northern Iowa Professor Larry Kelsey's astronomy classes, but each night in the campground he conducted star-gazing sessions.

RAGBRAI-XVI, 1988

The ride had someone registered from every state in the union except Rhode Island. Offenburger discovered this and got on the phone to Rhode Island officials urging them to send a representative, expenses paid. A competition of some sort was held and Malcolm Starr, a banker, was selected. When Gov. Terry Branstad asked him why he thought he had been chosen, Starr said, "Well, I have a few gray hairs." He said he was having a wonderful time and hoped to come back the next year with more people from Rhode Island.

I'm not sure he came back the next year, but he did return for sure in 1997 for RAGBRAI's twenty-fifth birthday. Starr wasn't the first person from Rhode Island to ride RAGBRAI. It just happened that no one applied from that state in 1988.

One of the more entertaining small-town acts came in Odebolt where four prominent businessmen—Jim Wareham, Larry Beckman, Howard Hustedt and Al Wilkie—call themselves "The Whistlers." They doffed their shirts, disguised their ample bellies as faces and held up garbage cans painted to appear as top hats. Their "facial" makeup included pursed "lips" drawn around their navels. They performed to music. The bikers loved it.

The overnight stop in Des Moines that year was one of the best. The riders were welcomed into the city through an archway, over a red carpet and handed paper black ties for the evening's entertainment. Marlene Anderson, chairwoman of entertainment for the city's effort, said the committee handed out 17,000 paper ties, and ran out by 3:30 p.m. with a lot of cyclists still out on the road. The lampposts all sported evening wear. There was plenty of food and plenty of drink. The vendors did extremely well and by evening Court Avenue was absolutely packed. but people did find a few square inches to dance on. It was a continuation of the street dance in Breda earlier in the week.

I wrote a piece eating crow, happily, saying "I can't remember a time when I was so happy to be proved wrong." I'd warned of disaster with camping on the Statehouse grounds. Not one of my predictions—from bicycle theft to violence—came to pass.

One of the last towns on this ride before ending in Fort Madi-

111

son was West Point. People there built a huge mound of bicycles with steps leading up the side. They called it Mount RAGBRAI. The city park overflowed with food stands and games and everything one would find at a fair. It wasn't the first pass-through town to make elaborate preparations, but it was one of the more creative ones. It seemed to begin the tradition of having the last town before an overnight town become the party center.

RAGBRAI-XVII, 1989

The ride started in Glenwood with the usual party, blessings of the mayor and dipping of the wheels in the Missouri. Unfortunately, the partyers left the town square an unholy mess of beer bottles and trash. This was partly because the town had chosen not to have an outdoor beer garden, but the mess came back to haunt RAGBRAI three years later.

On this ride, and only for the second time in the history of RAGBRAI, there was an act of vandalism against the riders. Someone spread roofing nails along a 14-mile stretch from north of Clarinda to north of U.S. 34 sometime before 5 a.m. Sgt. Frank Fisher of the state patrol, who was RAGBRAI safety coordinator at the time, discovered them. Clarinda and Montgomery County sent in street sweepers that worked the road to Stanton and back. But many riders ended up with one or more flat tires.

In Atlantic the chamber hosted a VIP dinner, but not the usual kind—politicians, athletes, entertainers and so on. These VIPs were selected at random from among the cyclists as they rode into town. The message here was that the real VIPs on RAGBRAI are the riders themselves. Thirty-five riders were handed letters designating them as VIPs and inviting them and their guests to a surprise celebrity dinner provided by Atlantic merchants. It was lots of fun for those chosen.

There was also a wedding in Atlantic. Kimberly Eggleston of Cedar Rapids and Michael Albers of Anamosa had met on RAG-BRAI the year before and decided it would be appropriate to get married on the next year's ride. The Chamber of Commerce of Atlantic provided an 8-foot-long cake and champagne.

Riders came upon a 1964 pink Cadillac parked on a flatbed trailer on the main street in Griswold, the seats removed and converted into a hot tub. Twenty-four men from Mount Ayr each had put up $100 for the contraption. It was quite an attraction.

Free Popsicles were given to all who wanted them in Bayard. Mike Deeth of Bayard, in charge of the Garst Seed Corn exhibit there that day, said he gave away 6,728, "But we missed a ton of riders, probably a good 3,000," he said.

By far the most memorable breakfast ever on RAGBRAI was hosted that year by the Randall Arts Council. There was valet parking for bikes, and waiters dressed in tuxes and black ties who served Belgian waffles and champagne sherbet. There was even a piano player. Another outstanding event on this ride happened in Cedar Falls. Outside the air-conditioned Unidome, where riders were welcome, 144 tentlike structures were set up on the campus for the riders. At night the entire complex was turned into a neon-light sculpture designed by Jim White, senior professor of sculpture at Arizona State University at Tucson. He titled it "Square Wave—Aere Perennius." Waves of lights swept over the tents, but when the occupant wanted to go to bed, the lights could be turned off.

At the end of a long windy next day the riders arrived in Dyersville. Many of them took the shuttle bus to the Field of Dreams, a place made famous by the movie, to watch and participate in some baseball games.

What many will remember is that Benson and I miscalculated the mileage for that day. The mileage was listed as 76 but it turned out to be 86. Worst of all, the day was very hot with a headwind. And when the riders reached the point where their odometers read 76 miles, they came upon a sign that said, "Dyersville 10 Miles." Many wanted to kill me, and I couldn't contradict the impulse. Last day, Dyersville to Bellevue, ended for the first time in a downpour.

One of our good friends, Linda Matson of Des Moines, created a small sensation by buying half a dozen plastic butts at a theatrical supply store in West Des Moines and recruiting a half-dozen of our other friends to wear them that day while cycling. Spectators did double takes and the jokes flew all day as they rode through the towns.

114

RAGBRAI-XVIII, 1990

This year's route went from Sioux Center to Burlington. By now the number was up to about 10,000 riders, coming from as far away as New Zealand and Denmark.

This was also the year the people in Algona tried to get into the *Guinness Book of Records* for the longest cake ever baked. It was six blocks long and every biker was welcome to a piece. It even tasted good.

Cedar Rapids had commissioned an enormous balloon sculpture of a bicycle rider in the camping area. Alas, on the day we rode into Cedar Rapids, wind and rain pretty much destroyed the sculpture. But from the balloons remaining in place one could see that it had been impressive.

The rain had turned much of the park grounds into mud, and several of the cyclists started a mud slide, a variation on the tavern beer slides that we RAGBRAI organizers deplore. The mud slide, however, ended in a tragic accident. Thomas Short, then 26, of Wheaton, Ill., broke his neck sliding and died two years later, a heavy price for an innocent act.

The macho way to end the ride that year was to ride down the hairpin turns of Snake Alley in Burlington. The cobblestones were slippery from the rain and there were a few spills, but none serious.

495 miles

RAGBRAI-XIX, 1991

This was Benson's last one as wagonmaster and Green's first and only as apprentice. The ride started in Missouri Valley and, as had been our practice for years, a bunch of us gathered Saturday morning at our house in Des Moines and drove over to the start in caravan.

Green had gone there the night before to give a hand to the local committee. Motorola had outfitted *The Register* crew with new, sophisticated two-way radios. Benson and Green each had one, and as soon as we got in range, they started talking to each other. We got closer and they kept talking. We drove into the campground area and we could see Green standing under a tree, and they kept talking. Finally, we got close enough for me to roll down a window and call out greetings to Green. And they were still talking on the radios.

That year's ride literally started with a bang, an actual rifle shot by a character dressed up as a frontiersman. Benson's send-off words of wisdom were, "Take no prisoners," a line originally used by Don Kaul.

Steve Roberts came with a computerized recumbent bike, one that could tell you anything at any time, could keep him in touch with his business and had cost a couple of million dollars. He rode that year but I don't remember seeing him after the start.

Many of the regulars were along: Paul Bernhard of Bancroft, the pork-chop man who could string out "Poooooork Chooooop" in his bass voice seemingly forever; Susie Burch and Lois Peterson, the route-marking mamas; and Sgt. Frank Fisher of the state patrol, serving as safety coordinator.

Years later, in a story about Burch and Peterson (who also was office manager and the "voice of RAGBRAI" to hundreds of riders for years), Peterson was quoted as saying, "People ask if I ride RAGBRAI. I always say, "Heavens no. That's the one week

115

of the year Susan and I can tell 8,000 people where to go and they don't mind."

The ride passed through towns noted for some famous or infamous characters and the towns made sure bikers knew about them. There were Bonnie and Clyde, who had robbed a bank in Stuart; John Wayne, born Marion Morrison in Winterset; Wyatt Earp, born in Pella; and the buildings that once housed Grant Wood, famous for his painting "American Gothic," and his art colony in Stone City.

Pella hosted a typical Dutch reception with its famous Dutch letters and other traditional pastries. Winterset tried for the longest peanut butter sandwich, 300 feet long, but it wasn't as successful as the longest cake of a previous ride.

Grinnell had an obstacles course for those inexperienced in driving a small front-end loader. The ride ended again at Bellevue, only two years after the first finish there. We returned that soon because the first visit had almost drowned in torrential rain. And Bellevue did us proud. There was a big party for Benson, a farewell. It was a surprise for him because the two Benson children and all the grandchildren were there. Daughter Nancy drove up from Des Moines and son Mark, a pilot in the Navy, flew up from Jacksonville, Fla., in a propeller-driven Navy trainer. Mark said he had to land five times for fuel.

RAGBRAI-XX, 1992

This was a big one, a RAGBRAI birthday, and Kaul came back for it in honor of its being the twentieth. We purposely brought the ride back to Des Moines, and again, as in 1988, routed the cyclists through Des Moines on Locust Street past the Register and Tribune building.

The ride began in Glenwood and ended in Keokuk with overnight stops in Shenandoah, Bedford, Osceola, Des Moines, Oskaloosa and Mount Pleasant.

Bungee jumping was having its 15 minutes of popularity at the time, and someone set up a bungee jumping rig in Glenwood. Quite a few cyclists began their ride with a big jump and a lot of bouncing at the end of a stout rubber band, then had a chance to reprise the leap in Des Moines, where another rig was set up on a bridge over the Des Moines River.

Glenwood also remembered 1989, when the cyclists littered the square with beer bottles, and got tough on public drinking. The police were out on the streets writing citations on anyone with an open beer in his hand. Some of the riders objected, but the streets were clean.

The first day, an inline skater slipped in among the riders for part of the day. In Shenandoah, Offenburger's home town, the Earl May company bused riders to its show gardens.

This was also the year that the Ride Right committee, headed by Tim Lane, got organized and worked hard to enhance the safety of the riders by promoting helmets, no drafting, no racing and riding on the right side of the road. The Ride Right organization is still working to accomplish these and many other cycling safety goals.

Bedford, at 1,459 population, was one of the smaller towns ever to host RAGBRAI, and it was one of the best organized.

The Schwinn bicycle company set up its exhibit of historic bicycles in Osceola, and to prove that one doesn't need a lightweight ten-speed, one rider rode RAGBRAI on a 1941 Schwinn.

Des Moines truly outdid itself in 1992 with a Wizard of Oz theme, yellow brick road and all. The characters were all present and played to a mob scene that evening down by the river. The Des Moines police, stars of the 1988 visit to Des Moines with their friendliness, were just as good this time. And one cyclist leading a group into Des Moines that day was none other than Des Moines Chief of Police Bill Moulder. His group was riding as "Team Pig."

This was also the year we began requiring all riders to sign a

117

waiver and release form. We've been doing it ever since, and have not yet suffered a lawsuit. Of course, we never suffered a lawsuit before requiring the waivers, either.

We had another wedding, probably the fourth on a RAGBRAI, when James Neagle and Bobbi Wilson of Cedar Rapids exchanged vows in Knoxville with their bike helmets on.

On the unhappy side, long-time RAGBRAI rider John Cazanas of Rockford suffered what was believed to be a stroke and a head injury after falling from his bike.

At the end of the ride in Keokuk, I got all the RAGBRAI principals present—Don and Jackie Benson, my wife Ann, Don Kaul, Chuck and Carla Offenburger and anyone else I could find—up on the stage at the ending ceremony, introduced all of them and described their RAGBRAI roles and said, "Take a good look at us, because if it weren't for us, you wouldn't be here."

It got a good laugh, but I meant it.

RAGBRAI-XXI, 1993

This was the year of the flood, the summer that Des Moines went 12 days without tap water.

Fortunately, we had chosen a northern route that year that avoided the worst-hit areas of the state—Sioux City to Dubuque, with overnight stops at Sheldon, Emmetsburg, Clarion, Osage, Decorah and Manchester. At one time, we had considered ending the ride that year in Muscatine. Good thing we didn't, because the riverfront ending area in Muscatine was still under water at the end of July.

As it was, the mud in the cornfields was one of the memories everyone took away from the 1993 ride. That and the areas of washouts. It was something to look down on the way into Emmetsburg and find a two-foot dropoff where only weeks before there had been a solid shoulder.

It was Sioux City's fourth time to host the ride's start, and by far the city's best reception ever, with a wide variety of entertainment including the usual fair-type attractions—fake sumo wrestlers, a concert by Dolly Parton, bands and food booths. Indeed, there was so much going on in Sioux City that Saturday night we all were amazed at the smoothness of the traffic. Besides the Parton concert and RAGBRAI, there was a semi-pro baseball game, reunions of all the city's high school classes and the annual Rivercade celebration was winding up.

Besides all that, on our Saturday in Sioux City part of Iowa Highway 4, our route into Emmetsburg two days away, was still under two inches of floodwater from the west branch of the Des Moines River. By the time we rode into Emmetsburg Monday afternoon, the highway was dry. In fact, except for a brief shower out of Emmetsburg and a downpour in the ending town of Dubuque, the week's weather was benevolent.

The overnight in Sheldon was the first ever for that community. Offenburger took a healthy ribbing from the locals for his 1981 pronouncement that Sheldon's high school sports nickname, the Orabs, was the worst in Iowa.

Along the way from Emmetsburg to Clarion people stopped to tour the West Bend Grotto, hit golf balls, eat, dance and visit with the locals. In one town there was a variation of the obstacle course: this time it was called the back-seat driver's contest. The driver was blindfolded and had to take directions from the sighted companion. Once again, lots of people went a bit out of their way to visit the Field of Dreams site in Dyersville on their way out of Manchester.

As noted above, the ride ended in a downpour in Dubuque.

RAGBRAI-XXII, 1994

This year's ride started for the third time in Council Bluffs and ended in Clinton with overnights in Harlan, Carroll, Perry, Marshalltown, Marion and Maquoketa. It was the first of two years that I rode our tandem with

Tucker Robinson, 10, the son of old friends of ours in Rochester, N.Y. I wrote in the July 24 *Sunday Register* that "I have no idea what he's going to learn in the course of this week, but I'm pretty sure it will be something he'll never forget. I imagine I'll learn a few things, too," and we both did.

Bill Zenor of Red Oak, a RAGBRAI legend who had been with the ride since 1974 as a state trooper and since retirement as an assistant first to Don Benson and then to Jim Green, had to miss this year's because of surgery scheduled the week of the ride. But he was at his son's house in Harlan the Sunday of the ride, visiting with the cyclists. "I'll be back next year," he said. "I like this crazy thing too much not to come back."

Dr. Greg Ganske of Des Moines, who won election to Congress that year, was along with his wife, Corrine, which was nothing new for a politician. What was new was that this year's was Ganske's sixth RAGBRAI. And we'd never known he cared.

Carl Voss of Des Moines, a legendary pie connoisseur had the quote of the week: "If you lose weight on RAGBRAI," he said, "you are not having a good time. I'm on the RAGBRAI See Food Diet. See it and eat it."

Every year, host communities wrestle with the question of where to put RAGBRAIers who want overnight accommodations somewhere other than the campground. Folks in Maquoketa came up with a couple of imaginative solutions. Myrna and Bob Larkey, who own Maquoketa Livestock Auction, volunteered the use of a horse barn for housing. It was clean and full of fresh hay, and had a restaurant and a large parking lot for recreational vehicles. As a result, some 200 cyclists stayed there. The other unusual solution came from florist Glenn Brock, who housed 60 campers in an empty greenhouse.

The week's weather was one of the best ever for RAGBRAI. The warmest day was Saturday coming into Clinton with temperatures in the mid-80s. There was only one day of scattered showers, humidity was low and winds favorable all week. "I don't know who put the fix in for the weather," said Bill

Scheitzach, 39, of LaCrosse, Wis., a veteran of 16 RAGBRAIs, "but they sure knew who to talk to."

And finally, Sara Sieker of Littleton, Colo., a retired first-grade teacher on her sixth or seventh RAGBRAI, she wasn't sure which, told me she had ridden the *Denver Post*'s Ride the Rockies in Colorado as a RAGBRAI warmup, but that a lot of Iowa's hills are harder. "I'm putting my bike away after this one," she said. "I've had it." So much for flat old Iowa.

RAGBRAI-XXIII, 1995

RAGBRAI made its debut appearance on 121 the Internet in 1995 at www.weather.net/rag-brai/ragbrai.html, and has been on the web ever since. This also was the first year that an accident insurance policy was included in the RAGBRAI fee.

The ride started again in Onawa, the fourth time, then overnighted in Lake View, Fort Dodge, Iowa Falls, Tama/Toledo, Sigourney and Coralville before ending in Muscatine.

Lake View had a real problem with rumor control. As Andy Meredith, general chairman for the town said, "We have no local cable TV channel, and no radio station." And the rumors? "That the state fire marshal had visited the town and said we would run out of water," Meredith said; "That Fort Dodge wasn't going to let RAGBRAI stay there," said Carol Roth, recording secretary; "Those bicyclists are going to take everything we own," Roth again; "That the Iowa 150 ride is going to Carroll because we're not good enough for them," Meredith again; "What are you going to do about the damage?" Roth. But everything turned out just fine.

Along the way from Lake View to Fort Dodge, the world's largest popcorn ball 2,225 pounds and 22 feet in circumference—was on display in Sac City (who said there's nothing to see in Iowa?).

Out-of-the-mouths-of-babes department: Nancy Dostal, publicity co-chairwoman in Tama/Toledo, took her daughter, Kelli, 12, to an evening when volunteers were inflating balloons to decorate the town, and Kelli said, "Gee, Mom, everyone in town is involved in this—old people, little kids and everybody." A RAGBRAI moment.

Thursday of RAGBRAI-XXIII, Tama/Toledo to Sigourney, was one of the most difficult in the ride's history. The day's route was mostly south, and the wind came up that day out of the south with gusts to 40 miles an hour. It even gave my wife a black eye. She was minding her own business, eating ice cream at a church food stop when a gust lifted a corner of a canopy releasing the two-by-four holding it up, which fell and hit her in the face. A fraction of an inch over and the injury would have been truly serious. The day became known as "Saggy Thursday," the name that was put on a special patch commemorating that wind.

After all that the cyclists rolled into Muscatine at the end of an easy, 47-mile day for the traditional dipping of the front wheels and the annual good-byes until next year.

RAGBRAI-XXIV, 1996

We returned to Sioux Center for this year and overnighted in Sibley, Estherville, Lake Mills, Charles City, Cresco and Fayette (the smallest town ever to host RAGBRAI at just 900-plus population when Upper Iowa University is on vacation) before finishing in Guttenberg.

One feature of the ride was an optional loop between Lake Mills and Charles City that turned a 72-mile route into a 150-mile day in honor of Iowa's sesquicentennial year. Astonishingly, more than 1,000 riders did the 150 miles (yes, I was among them).

The weather for the week was the most perfect ever for a RAGBRAI—winds out of the northwest all week and daytime temperatures that never climbed out of the low 80s. In addition, there were virtually no challenging hills until the last day and a half.

The RAGBRAI staff underwent one major change in 1996. Ray Reasoner who had driven a sag wagon on the ride for 16 years decided it was time to get out of the air-conditioned van and onto a bike. "I've been saying for 10 years that I'm going to do this," said Reasoner, then 62, a farmer and accountant, "and I decided this year was it." Kay Reasoner, then 57, an insurance secretary and Ray's wife, again drove a sag wagon—a 15-passenger van pulling trailers for bicycles—for her 17th year in a row.

The first day's ride into Estherville took the cyclists past Ocheyedan Mound, jutting 170 feet above the pancake-flat terrain around it. For years it was thought to be the highest point in Iowa until a new survey in 1971 determined the high point actually is in a hog lot near Sibley.

In Lake Mills, Gov. Terry Branstad, a native of the town, was in the middle of the main street, greeting riders as they arrived. Branstad has ridden all of one RAGBRAI and a couple of days of a few others. He was bemoaning his lack of time to do another one.

Charles City, home of a Sara Lee bakery, gave away close to 10,000 pieces of apple pie to riders as they entered town. The pie was especially welcome to 150-mile loopers, many of whom were close to bonking by the time they reached Charles City.

In Cresco, I sought out Tom Barnes, RAGBRAI chairman there, who told me a tale to gladden a RAGBRAI planner's heart. A Cresco native, Barnes said that when he was growing up, everyone in town knew each other. But in the last 15 or so years, the town's economy changed from agricultural to light industrial, a lot of new people moved in and while the natives were friendly they still thought of the new people as, well, new people. Then, RAGBRAI came along and posed organizational demands unlike any other the town had ever seen. "What RAG-

123

BRAI has done," Barnes said, "is what I hoped it would do—bring the town together." He told of a woman who had volunteered for a committee, saying that she hoped it would help her become a part of the community. Then, not many weeks later, as she was leaving a meeting, he heard her say, "I now feel like a Crescoite." I told him, "You're going to make me cry," and he responded, "I almost did."

The day from Cresco to Fayette went through the Czech towns of Protivin and Spillville, where the riders devoured kolaches (Czech pastries) by the gross.

124   For challenges, however, no RAGBRAI town ever has faced a bigger one than did Fayette. Bringing 12,000 people into a town of 910 for an overnight stay is, on the face of it, an outrageous proposition. The rumor of the day among the cyclists was that Fayette would run out of food. "I hope we do run out of food," said Mike Simon, food committee co-chairman, "as soon as everyone is fed." He added that the town, with Upper Iowa University's help, of course, was prepared to serve 14,000 dinners. The visit went extremely well, the hospitality was great and except for a few whines about entertainment space, everyone went away happy the next day for the big finish in Guttenberg.

One highlight of the week was the participation of 130 members of the U.S. Air Force, plus the then-secretary of the Air Force, Sheila Widnall, and the Night Wing Air Force Band.

It was, indeed, a RAGBRAI to remember.

RAGBRAI-XXV, 1997

Another year, another birthday, this time the twenty-fifth.

And the weather on this one was as bad as the weather was good the year before. In fact, I have no doubt that the weather on RAGBRAI-XXV was the worst, the most difficult the ride has ever experienced. The humidity was in the 90s the entire week. And it was hot, hotter, hottest. Overcast skies through the middle of the week, and a drizzle at least one morning helped, but then the sun came out with ferocity Thursday afternoon and stayed out all day Friday and Saturday.

There were places on the road at the bottoms of hills and in sheltered areas untouched by breezes where the temperature had to be well above 100 degrees.

The route was no help. The first day, Missouri Valley to Red Oak, was 82 miles of unrelenting hills. The rest of the route went mainly through southern Iowa, overnighting after Red Oak in Creston, Des Moines, Chariton, Bloomfield and Fairfield and ending in Fort Madison.

I knew it was a difficult route from the start, writing in the February announcement story, "This year's route could be characterized as the answer to a masochist's dream—it is guaranteed to make strong men weep, strong women stronger and young children old." And that was before anyone knew anything about the weather.

Then along came Rich Ketchum, a computer wiz, with graphs of each day's route showing the daily changes in elevation. He put them on our RAGBRAI web page. Wow. The total vertical climbing for the week, according to Ketchum's figures (the data came from the U.S. Geological Survey) was 14,493 feet, just a tad under three miles. Let's hear it again for good old flat Iowa.

The first day was everything we expected it to be, and more. Tough. The sag wagons, which usually quit by 6 p.m., ran past 9 that day.

Red Oak had declared Sunday Bill Zenor Day in honor of the former state trooper who had worked on RAGBRAI for so many years (and still does).

Paul Bernhard of Bancroft, known to RAGBRAIers for years as Mr. Pork Chop, showed up with a new paint job on his old school bus—pink, with a pig's snout painted on the front, ears on the front corners of the roof and a curly tail on the rear.

U.S. Representative Greg Ganske of Des Moines was back (he'd been riding RAGBRAI long before he got into politics) and listening to music on earphones. "Vivaldi," he said. "With all these hills, I needed something with a beat."

Creston was typical of all the smaller towns on this week's ride; that is, they all went all out to spruce up their communities, painting this, tuck-pointing that, putting up welcome banners and so on. "The cool thing," said Creston co-chair Chris Duree, "is that the people were driving around last night as if they were looking at Christmas lights, and everyone agreed the town has never looked better."

Budget restrictions kept Des Moines from putting on the kind of reception that it had in the past. RAGBRAI came in from the south and stayed at the south edge of Des Moines at the zoo and on the grounds of the old Fort Des Moines. There was plenty of food and entertainment (a laser light show put on by *The Register* was one event), but the celebration was on the restrained side.

The next day's ride finally accomplished something we've hoped to do for years—stay overnight in Chariton and pass  through every county in the state. Lucas was the last county on the list, and Chariton is in Lucas County. That day's ride turned out to be the pleasantest of the week, although the humidity was still at a ghastly level. The town looked great and the welcome was greater. Almost two miles of the road into town was lined on both sides with small American flags. Best of all, 5,000 handmade candy turtles were donated by Piper's store of Chariton and handed out by volunteers.

If anything, things got even better in Bloomfield, another community whose small size made hosting RAGBRAI a real challenge. Land of Oz was the town's theme, and someone had actually managed to mount a many colored cloth rainbow on the county courthouse. As a bonus, many of the riders stopped at

126

Amish farms on the road to Bloomfield where families had set up food stands.

The day's ride, however, was brutal. The century loop was a beautiful route around Lake Rathbun, but the sun came out in the afternoon and simply baked everyone. Again, the sag wagons worked overtime hauling exhausted and dehydrated cyclists into town.

Fairfield's reception was as good as the weather was bad. In fact, towns all along the route were exceptionally well prepared.

On the last day into Fort Madison, West Point again had built its "Mount RAGBRAI" out of junk bicycles welcoming the riders. The heat continued, but failed to wilt Fort Madison hospitality. On the way to dipping their wheels, cyclists rode down to the Mississippi under an arch of 50 bikes built by Rich Mohrfeld.

One popular innovation of the week were the small blue "passports" provided to all registered riders by the U.S. Postal Service, a RAGBRAI sponsor for the first time. Riders took the books to post offices along the route to have them stamped. There were lines all week at post offices across the state.

And finally, two longtime RAGBRAIers finally got their chance to participate as riders. Lt. Darrell Cox and Sgt. Frank Fisher had worked on RAGBRAI as safety control directors a combined total of 12 years. This time, they got to see it from bicycle seats, and they said they had a great time.

RAGBRAI Personalities Stories,

anecdotes, people, personalities, memories flooding

back, some funny, some full of pathos, some downright

sentimental.

So herewith, some of the people, tales and hijinks that have made so many RAGBRAIs so memorable for me and Ann.

Why not start with Big Al Culbert, then of Charles City, on that fateful RAGBRAI night in 1983 in Clarion?

Culbert, a veteran of many RAGBRAIs, was tenting on school grounds with his son, Kevin, then 22 and a student at the University of Iowa. Big Al's two daughters, Ann, 18, and Teresa, 15, were camped a couple of tents away. Al had gone to bed at a reasonable hour. Kevin was still out.

As the evening wore on, Al recalled recently, the campground quieted down as it usually does. Sometime in the middle of the night he awoke to hear the tent door zipper open and close, and rolled over and went back to sleep.

Then about 5 a.m. or so, he woke up, rolled over expecting to see his son, and saw instead a young woman. "I think you described her in your story as of a blonde persuasion," he said. He didn't know what to do. He unzipped the tent and called a friend over to take a look. Finally, he woke her up and said something like, "Young lady, do you *really* want to be in this tent?"

He continued, "She woke up, her eyes as big as saucers, and it's a good thing I'd left the tent open because I think she would have gone right through the door." Son Kevin rode again on RAGBRAI-XXV with his wife and was planning to return in 1998, Al said. Kevin is now a physician, a major in the Air Force.

"You know," Al added, "he never *has* told me where the hell he spent that night."

Huck Thompson

Only one person has ridden every mile of every RAGBRAI from the start in 1973 through the 25th in 1997, including all the century loops, the 150-mile loop in 1996, plus untold side trips to towns a mile or so off the route for refueling and an occasional beer.

His name is Frank (better known as Huck) Thompson. He worked in the mail room at *The Register* for 36 years from 1961 to 1997, then became business agent for Teamsters Union Local 90 in Des Moines.

A Florida native, Thompson ran track and was a speed roller skater into middle age. "Until it got too tough trying to keep up with those 18-year-olds," he told Chuck Offenburger in a 1992 interview. Looking for another sport, he tried ice hockey but quit when a puck hit him in the mouth, loosening several teeth, and took up bicycling instead.

I became aware of Huck in the early '70s at a fund-raiser bike ride at the State Fairgrounds. It was a 50-mile ride around a loop on the grounds, and what impressed me about Thompson was his speed. He finished the 50 miles in about half my time.

"I'd been doing a little riding back in the late '60s and early '70s," he told Offenburger. "And then one day at work, John Karras came down and said he and Don Kaul were going to try to ride their bikes all the way across Iowa and wondered if I'd like to go along. I thought about it for five minutes and then went right in and put in for vacation."

He's been RAGBRAIing ever since. But it wasn't until the mid-80s, he said, that he and others began talking about the dwindling number of cyclists who had ridden every RAGBRAI

130

mile. Then, in 1990, the RAGBRAI planners held a dinner for those who had been on all the rides up to that time. Ann and I were included even though each of us had missed one ride. Our justification was that each of us had done a make-up RAGBRAI for the one we missed. There were 22 of us, and as we talked, it became clear that Thompson was the only one who hadn't missed a single mile.

He has seen it all, Soggy Monday in 1981, Saggy Thursday in 1995, torrential downpours, heat, cold, the endless hills of southern Iowa, the Alps of northeastern Iowa and all the beautiful scenes and weather, too.

The closest he ever came to quitting, however, occurred in 1991 when he had a touch of food poisoning or the flu the first three days of RAGBRAI XIX.

"I know there were a couple of days there when I probably shouldn't have been riding," he said. "But I had a couple of guys in our group ride right alongside of me and keep their eyes on me. We made it. After all these years of never missing a mile, there's only one way I'm not riding—if I'm dead."

His best memories?

"No single thing," he said. "Just talking to the people in the towns. Once in a barber shop everyone wanted to know everything about the ride."

Thompson was 61 in 1998. He's a little slower than he was in 1972, but just as strong.

The other 21 who had ridden in all the RAGBRAIs through XVII were Scott Dickson, now of Ohio; Rick Paulos of Cedar Rapids and his mother, Margaret, of Davenport; Gary Mohler of West Burlington; James and Nancy Hopkins of Des Moines and her parents, Mr. and Mrs. Floyd Gustafson of Walnut, Ill; Marvin Rohden of Gowrie; Robert Hudson of Stratford; Greg Schmidt, a.k.a. Frank Iowa, of Iowa City; Carter LeBeau of Davenport; Leon and Avonelle Moss of rural Madrid; Bill Albright, Thomas Dreyer, Don and Lois Hartline and Ann and I, all of Des Moines, and Don Benson (the old wagonmaster) of Clive.

131

Of those, all have continued attending RAGBRAI through XXV except the Gustafsons, who quit after XXIV; Rohden who stopped at XVIII; the Mosses who made it through XXIV; and Benson, who resigned at the end of the 1991 ride but returned at least once to help his successor, Jim Green. I was unable to find Gary Mohler.

There were many other RAGBRAI regulars, of course. Prominent among them were John (Pat) Dorrian, former mayor of Des Moines, and his wife, Carolyn. He joined the ride for the first time in 1986 with his son. Then, he and Carolyn rode a tandem on RAGBRAI 1989 through 1996, missing 1993 because of flooding in Des Moines. As mayor, Dorrian was instrumental in planning the tremendously successful RAGBRAI overnights in Des Moines in 1988 and 1992, when the downtown was packed with people.

Carter LeBeau and Friends

I'll never forget my first sight of Carter LeBeau. It was in Davenport, Iowa. He was dressed in many colored, patchwork walking shorts of quilt-like construction and standing on a flatbed truck-trailer, waving his arms and yelling. He had organized a century ride, the first ever for the Quad-Cities Bicycle Club, one of the older organized clubs in Iowa.

Ann and I had driven over from Des Moines to ride in it. If memory serves, we had never before ridden 100 miles in one day.

Anyway, there was Carter, up there on the flatbed, a little bike cap perched on the back of his head, yelling directions at everyone. He also was wearing his silly socks—knee-highs with horizontal stripes of many colors. He was quite a sight.

What appealed to me about Carter from that first sight of him was his relentless enthusiasm for life and all its wonders. He oozes enthusiasm. Things are terrific, thank you, and let's grab each day by the throat and enjoy it to the fullest.

He has been on at least part of every RAGBRAI from the beginning in 1973, one of only a dozen or so people who have been.

132

He got into cycling after moving to Iowa in 1963 from Chicago. A friend talked him into taking a weekend ride in Wisconsin. Carter rode it on the bike he had at the time, a three-speed J.C. Higgins, and, he said, "fell in love with biking."

Then, in 1972, the year before RAGBRAI began, he and a friend decided to ride across Wisconsin. They had such a good time they made a pact to ride across a different state every year. The next year, when Kaul and I announced our ride across Iowa, Carter called his friend and told him their cross-state ride was already planned for them.

They rented a car, bought a cheap bike rack, drove to Sioux City and cycled back to Davenport. "RAGBRAI got me into bike riding big time," Carter told me.

He and another friend, Bob Frey, founded the Quad-Cities Club's Tour of the Mississippi River Valley in 1976, a very popular two-day ride from Scott County, Iowa, to Dubuque and back. The twenty-first TOMRV was held in 1998.

Carter also has taken many extended tours. He's ridden across the entire United States at least three times and across sections of the nation many others.

His closest cycling friends in the early years of RAGBRAI were John Keane of Moline, who worked for IBM, and Frey, a Moline dentist. They were, to put it as gently as possible, an odd trio.

Keane was as quiet a liberal Democrat as LeBeau was a noisy conservative Republican, yet, they got along famously.

They rode across the country one summer, just the two of them, mostly on the 1976 Bikecentennial route. Afterward, Carter would tell how he was messy and Keane was neat. "You'd come into the motel, Keane had already taken his shower and you couldn't tell which towel he'd used."

Frey was the comedian of the group. He had a belt he used to put on for special occasions. It had red blinkers over each of his love handles. They were directional signals, with a switch on the buckle that he could manipulate to make the left or right one blink.

133

He had to have weighed close to 300 pounds in those early years and couldn't have been much over six feet. He also was a dedicated beer drinker. I remember on one long, extremely difficult RAGBRAI day hearing LeBeau say, "You know this has to be a serious day. It's noon and Frey hasn't had a beer yet."

One year Frey, still closing in on 300 pounds, bought and brought on RAGBRAI an 18-pound titanium bike. It occurred to me at the time that there were better areas than his bike where he could have pared weight, but said nothing.

Each evening, when Frey was off drinking beer, one of his friends would remove the seat post from the frame and pour a handful of lead shot down the seat tube. By the end of the week, the bike weighed close to 30 pounds and Frey was wondering why he was having so much trouble on the hills.

One of the many RAGBRAI traditions is a closing ceremony in the early afternoon of the last day in the ending town. Carter usually attends, and at some time during the proceeding he usually shouts, "Fifty-one weeks 'til RAGBRAI."

He also gets a photograph of me every year eating watermelon.

And he tells stories, most of them true. He told of riding off the route with some friends one year to go to Okoboji, then catching up with RAGBRAI the next day. That meant cycling through a couple of towns the ride had been through the day before. Carter's group stopped at a cafe for breakfast, only to hear a farmer exclaim, "Oh, my God, they're coming back."

Ben Davidson

At 6 feet 8 inches and 250 pounds, with a gravelly voice that cuts through the cacophonous noise level of any jam-packed small-town bar, Ben Davidson rarely gets lost in a crowd, as hosts of RAGBRAIers know.

Davidson played professional football from 1961 to 1974, and was an all-pro defensive end with the Oakland Raiders in the team's glory years from 1964 to 1973. He first attended RAG-

BRAI in 1987 and has been on the ride 10 times from then through 1997.

He missed 1994 when he went on an expenses-paid trip to Barcelona, Spain, the same week as RAGBRAI. He went with 31 other former Raiders at the invitation of Al Davis, then the Raiders owner, to watch the team play the Denver Broncos.

"There's a famous walk in Barcelona called "Las Ramblas," Davidson told me recently. "So that year I traded Las Ramblas for Iowa cornfields."

Davidson had heard of an Iowa bike ride but doesn't know where or when. Then, in the fall of 1986, he was playing in a Variety Club of Iowa golf tournament with Rick Jurgens, now senior vice president, chief administrative officer, at Hy-Vee, Inc., when Jurgens asked if Davidson had heard of RAGBRAI.

"Rick asked me if I'd like to ride in it," Davidson said. "I said I'd love to. And he said, 'Okay, okay.' And I said, 'Okay what?' And he said, 'You're all set.'"

So Davidson went home to La Mesa, Calif., got an application in the mail, filled it out, sent it in, then got a rejection notice and was told to try again next year. "Then Rick, being the person he is, followed up by calling and asking if I was in. I told him I got rejected, and he said, 'No, no. I'll fix it up,' and I don't know what he did or who he talked to but the next thing I knew I got wrist bands and all that in the mail and started riding. I'd been a bicycle rider since I was a kid."

After college, Davidson briefly played football for the New York Giants, the Green Bay Packers, and the Washington Redskins before beginning what he calls "my long and fruitful sojourn with the Oakland Raiders.

"I had a lot of fun and played on some great teams. One good record we still have is best record over a 3-year period, 37-4-1. We lost four over three years and played in Super Bowl II." The Raiders didn't win a Super Bowl while he was there but went on to win three others later.

He said that after his first RAGBRAI in 1987, he went home

and talked so much about it that his wife, Kathy, said, "Wait a minute, that sounds like too much fun. I'm going with you next time." And she did and has been back many times, as have been both of his brothers and his daughter.

He also has been back to Des Moines many times to participate in the annual Variety Club telethon raising money for Blank Children's Hospital. The 1998 telethon at the end of February was his eleventh. He still is associated with Miller beer (he was one of the former football players in those Miller Lite commercials several years ago) and has been invited to Des Moines each year by the Miller distributor there.

I've seen Davidson on RAGBRAI many times, but the most memorable occurred in 1995 when I was riding our tandem bicycle with my good friend Tucker Robinson, 11 years old at the time, of Rochester, N.Y.

Tucker was wearing a Miami Dolphins shirt because he's a Dolphins fan, when Davidson rode up and I introduced them.

"Where'd you get that silly Dolphins shirt, Tucker," Davidson said. "I used to play for the Raiders. We didn't like the Dolphins." Pause. "We didn't like anybody."

Then Davidson went into what has become his stock answer to the question, "Why do you go to Iowa?"

"I tell 'em I go for the variety," he boomed. "Sometimes there's corn on the left and soybeans on the right, sometimes there's soybeans on the left and corn on the right, and sometimes there's corn on both sides."

What did Tucker think of Davidson?

"He sure is big," Tucker said.

Noel Brown

I met Noel Brown in 1974 as we approached Camp Dodge north of Des Moines near the end of a brutally hot day's ride from Guthrie Center. It was obvious he was not having a good time.

I'm guessing that Noel was in his 50s at the time. He was

short, perhaps 5-2, bowlegged, Irish as could be (as you learned with his first words), red-faced, very sunburned and totally out of sorts under his pork-pie hat. I learned later that he lived in Iowa City and was a psychiatrist.

So what else could I do but strike up a conversation with him and try to cheer him up?

"What brought you on this bike ride?" I asked, thinking at the time that this bike ride was about the last place in the world he should have been.

"Ah, there lies a tale," he said, or words to that effect. "The boys did it."

He had three sons, all pre-teens.

"The wife and I went out to dinner on our anniversary (you have to imagine the Irish brogue in all of this) and we came home and had drinks in front of the fire and were feeling real mellow and relaxed when in crept the little sons-of-bitches and said, 'Dad, can we go on the bike ride?' and I said, 'Sure, why not?' and here I am."

Brown was known to knock back a few as he rode. I remember riding with him and talking one morning when he broke off at the sight of a Budweiser sign and said, "Ah, John, there's me lemonade stand," and went off for a drink.

And that habit got him into trouble with Trooper Bill Zenor.

In his early years as RAGBRAI safety coordinator, Zenor would change out of his uniform into street clothes at the end of the day, and make the last sweep back along the route with Don Benson, making certain no one having difficulty was left stranded out there. In 1976, they drove back as far as Thornburg and found Noel Brown by himself.

Driving farther back, they came upon his three sons. Benson and Zenor asked the boys what they were doing out on the road so late. They said they were waiting for their father. Zenor asked where he was and the boys said he was in a tavern. Zenor went ballistic.

137

They packed the boys and bikes into the van and found Brown. Bill "sort of explained to Noel" that those boys shouldn't be out there alone, Benson told me. "And that started the rift between Noel and Bill."

The next year, Benson said, Brown and Zenor kind of made up. One of the boys got in trouble one night. Benson and Zenor went to see the Browns, and Brown demonstrated to Zenor's satisfaction that he really was a disciplinarian and cared for his sons. They later became good friends.

For many years, Brown's wife would meet us in the parking lot at the end of the ride and produce bottles of champagne for a kind of tailgate celebration. After that first year, Brown became something of a dedicated cyclist, getting in shape each year for RAGBRAI. "It saved my life," he said once.

James and Nancy Hopkins and Family

Dr. James Hopkins and his wife, Nancy, of Des Moines, have been on every RAGBRAI since the first one in 1973. He is a pediatric surgeon, and cycles. Nancy drives the support vehicle. Her parents Mr. and Mrs. Floyd Gustafson of Walnut, Ill., used to go along and Floyd cycled the route through his 85th year, and was along but not cycling in 1997. He was 87 in 1998.

So what? you say, and I respond that the real point of this is that since the beginning, RAGBRAI has been this family's only vacation year after year after year. And it still is. Even the Hopkins children used to ride.

The family originally is from Walnut, Ill. James and Nancy came to Des Moines in 1967 after he finished his residency training. They moved back to Illinois in 1989–1991 because, James said, he had become too busy in Des Moines and went to Illinois to enter a partnership. Then the hospital where he worked in the Chicago area was sold to a for-profit corporation, his partner retired and he and Nancy moved back to Des Moines.

What about favorite RAGBRAI memories? There are so many, he said. "Probably the ice-cold showers."

And another one:

It was at the end of your talk just before the people left the Sioux City parking lot.

There was this loud bang, and you commented, "There's the first flat of the ride." And it was my son, Bill. He was 13 years old, and his tire blew. He ran over to Bill Albright's truck and got a tube, and one of the boys nearby helped him change the tire.

Bill rode about every mile of the ride until he left the state about six years after that. He's now an engineer with Boeing, builds airplanes, but he also likes to build bicycles. He built a bike for his grandfather about '89 or '90, a beautiful three-speed bike.

I also remember many if not most RAGBRAIs for interruptions to go back and take care of my little patients. And almost all of the routes had some of my former patients, and they would ask us to come by and say hello, so I had plenty of people I could kibbutz with. And that's what gave us the vacation part of it.

But come on, now, James. Are you sure you've never taken any other vacations besides RAGBRAI?

"Oh, gosh," he said, "we really don't take many vacations in my work."

Okay, if it works for them it certainly works for me.

Jon Riggs

A young man came along on SAGBRAI in 1974 who redefined the concept of physical disabilities for everyone who saw him.

Jon Riggs, 20, was a junior in fisheries and wildlife biology at Iowa State University, Ames, that year. He caused a minor sensation on the road because he had lost his right leg at the hip to bone cancer at the age of nine, but still was able to pedal up the southern Iowa hills faster than most.

139

Because of the "handicap," which he probably would have denied, and with good reason, he had to pedal in a true circular motion, pulling up as strongly as he pushed down.

There were three or four teen-age boys riding with me that week, and in an effort to keep the level of boredom down, I had them playing biking games, such as pretending a dog was going to chase us as far as the third telephone pole down the road.

Seeing Riggs on the road one morning, I suggested to the kids that all of us see what it would be like to pedal as he had to. So we all took one foot out of the toe clip, pulled the strap up tight on the other, locking that foot to the pedal, and tried to climb a hill. I made it part way up. Three of the teenagers got a little farther before having to give up. Only one of our number, Alan Kissane of Grinnell, then 15 and a very strong rider, made it to the top of the hill.

On another day, I was following about a quarter of a mile behind Riggs when I saw him suddenly and inexplicably pitch off the bike to the right and fall into the roadside ditch. As I came abreast of him and before I even had time to call out, he came up out of the ditch holding the left crank arm of his bicycle. The incredible strength of his one leg had stressed the steel spindle to the point that it had broken off.

Concerning his so-called disability, I found Riggs playing Frisbee using one crutch at the campground one evening. He was able to leap respectably high off that one leg and catch the Frisbee.

Asked if there was anything he wanted to do but couldn't because of being an amputee, he said there was nothing.

"When I first started to swim," he said, "I tipped over. But now I swim all the time."

When I last heard from him several years ago, he was working with the Department of Natural Resources in Minnesota.

He was an inspiration to a lot of people the year or two that he rode RAGBRAI.

Brian Wistey

Riggs is only one of many with physical disabilities who have attended RAGBRAI.

Another is Brian Wistey, who has been cycling across Iowa regularly since 1977. A motorcycle accident in July of 1967 "basically left me with a piece of my heel on the right foot," he said recently. His left foot was fine, but the right foot was essentially gone and one hand was broken. He wears a plastic prosthesis in place of a right foot. Aside from a slight limp, he hardly appears discomfited at all.

Brian told me he took up bicycling after he graduated from the University of Iowa in 1976, and started going on RAGBRAI in 1977. He has done 14 of them since then.

His only real difficulty, he said, "is getting up the hills. I don't do hills as fast as other people, but if I'm in halfway decent shape I can keep up on the flats. It's kind of tough for us one-legged fat men to get up the hills."

He has been riding from the start with a group called Team Lanning, named for Jim Lanning, who built bike frames for many of the group. Most of them are West Des Moines volunteer firemen, and, Wistey said with a laugh, many by now are retired. Randy Bracken is the fire chief, and all the rest are volunteers. Lanning himself has cycled on every RAGBRAI beginning in 1977.

What about memories, Brian?

Well, there was that RAGBRAI moment in Manchester in 1983 that the RAGBRAI organizers weren't supposed to hear about but did, when one of the members got drunk and out of hand and the scene threatened to become ugly, so some other members pinned him down and got him cuffed and off to the local jail for his own protection.

Some of the members wondered what they would do with the guy the next day. The hell with him, the word came back. Let him find his own way.

He was released the next morning, Wistey told me, found his own way to Dubuque and rode back to Des Moines very quietly. They did transport his gear to Dubuque for him. It was, after all, the couth thing to do.

Other memories?

"Yes. Number One, ending in Lansing in '77 after that magnificent downhill. Knowing that I had done it. One of the first things I was going to do when I got back to Des Moines was buy a helmet. I did and I've been wearing it ever since."

Among others, one of the most pleasant was the advent of the first portable showers ever brought on RAGBRAI. "Another one was feeling cocky because we had the first Ryder truck, and we were really easy to spot in the campground. That lasted about one year."

Another was when his two daughters went on RAGBRAI. It was very memorable for them. They both learned they could do it. Of course, each of them had a little crying jag along the way.

"RAGBRAI was kind of like a family reunion there for about 10 years," Wistey said. "One of the funniest realizations, as the group grew older, we remembered we used to camp at the corner of action and action, and now we're looking for the corner of quiet and quiet. In Osceola, for example, we camped at the East Park, about two miles from town. The younger people in the group complained that by the time they walked down there it was time to walk back."

Bill Albright

Bill's Cyclery, operated by Bill Albright and his wife, Takeko, was the first bike shop in Des Moines catering primarily to adults. Bikes were still thought of mainly as toys for kids when Albright opened his store in 1972. To that point, about the only 10-speed bikes readily available were those made by Schwinn of Chicago and those made by Raleigh of England. Albright brought in bicycles from France and Italy, Motobecanes, Gitanes, Peugots and Colnagos. Esoteric stuff.

He went on the first cross-Iowa ride in 1973 primarily because he wanted to ride it. Along the way, however, he established his shop among cyclists on the ride as the premier shop in Iowa. There were similar shops at the time in Grinnell, Cedar Falls, the Quad Cities, Ames and Iowa City, but Bill was the only one with a repair stand and spare parts on that first ride. And he sat outside his motel room each night until midnight repairing bikes. People came to believe that Bill's Cyclery was, indeed, "the enthusiasts' shop."

Albright looked a lot like Paul Stookey of Peter, Paul and Mary, fairly long hair springing out from a mainly bald pate. And he had a way of scrunching up his eyes when about to deliver a wry comment or the punch line of a joke.

143

Indeed, Albright had a most confusing habit when telling a joke. He'd sit cross-legged on the ground, spin out the joke and then, just before delivering the punch line, would scrunch up his eyes, grin and bend over touching his nose almost to the ground and deliver the line into the ground in a way that no one could hear it.

Actually, his way of telling a joke usually was a lot funnier than the joke itself.

Another amusing practice of Albright's was his way of paying a check in a cafe. He would take the check and his money in one hand and extend it to the person at the cash register, usually a woman. Then, when she took the end he was extending, he would hang onto it. Then, with both of them tugging at the check and bills, he would scrunch up his eyes, grin his grin and say, "This includes a generous gratuity."

His business practices were equally surprising. More than once I have gone into his shop and found him lying down on the floor behind the showcase, presumably catching a little nap.

He and Takeko sold the shop in February of 1997. Until then, though, they always showed up on RAGBRAI as one of the 14 or 15 official shops. And he had cycled all but about the last three.

Albright started cycling in the middle 1960s with the YMCA Bicycle Club under the leadership of veteran cyclist Ed Pugsley. There's a bronze plaque in the basement of the Des Moines YMCA with the names of those who completed the club's first ever 100-mile ride. Albright had a four-speed Sturmey-Archer Raleigh bike at the time.

Ann and I did a lot of cycling in addition to RAGBRAI in the '70s with a group of friends that included Albright. We had a lot of good times.

144 **Paul Bernhard**

They call him Mr. Pork Chop, and it's no joke. Nor is it meant as a derogatory term. Paul Bernhard has earned the title as surely as if he had been knighted by the Queen of England.

He and his crew have become fixtures on RAGBRAI. One sees the signs a long way off. A plume of white smoke rising from a spot over the hill and down the road can mean only one thing: As soon as the rider draws near, he will hear the clarion roar of Bernhard or one of his agents crying, "Pooooooooooooork Choooooooooooop."

Yes, Mr. Pork Chop is back.

It started in 1982 when RAGBRAI went through the tiny northern Iowa town of Bancroft, Bernhard's hometown. Bernhard at the time was president of both the Iowa Pork Producers and the Kossuth County Pork Producers associations.

He had his barbecue pits set up on a vacant lot in town. The pork producers barbecued what Bernhard had named the Iowa Chop—a cut of meat an inch and a half thick—over charcoal and corn cobs. They took an hour, and each time they were turned they were basted with melted butter.

That first year, the chops went for $1 apiece and a pint of beer was 50 cents. Talk about deals. Bernhard once told me that "One guy from Davenport got there early, before any were ready. He waited around and before he left he'd eaten five of them."

Bernhard and his crew have been selling his chops on every RAGBRAI starting in 1985.

He was honored by Bancroft when RAGBRAI went through town again in 1996 with a "Mr. Pork Chop Day." Mayor Lamont Jansen called Bernhard to the stage set up downtown and formally declared the day. Bernhard said, "Well, I don't speak much, so how about we all do the Pork Chop call instead."

And they did, several thousand of them assembled, screaming in unison, "Pooooooork Choooooooop."

Comedian Tom Arnold, a native of Ottumwa and perhaps best known as the former husband of Roseanne, was in town at the time, and Bernhard challenged him to join in. "Tom," said Bernhard, "I think you're probably too much of a wimp to call 'Pork Chop' with me," to which Arnold replied, "Hey, I was married to Roseanne for five years, so I don't think you can be calling me a wimp."

Not only was Bernhard honored by the town, he also expanded his normal crew, set up extra grills and sold 2,500 chops, his all-time best day.

The Odd Couple

For several years I've written a daily feature for *The Register* during the week of the bike ride titled "Postcard From RAGBRAI." I try each day to find a short story that I hope will elicit a chuckle or perhaps a tug at the heartstrings or some other reaction from readers.

Here is one of my favorites, from the July 24, 1992, *Register:*

A RAGBRAI couple: Vada Gibson of Marion, Ohio, and Bill Meyer of Gillett, Wis., started riding RAGBRAI together in 1978 and, having missed a couple for various reasons, are doing their 13th this year on a tandem. On at least one RAGBRAI past, Bill drove their vehicle each day to the next overnight town, then cycled back along the route until he met Vada and rode in with her. They also have biked together—

mostly on organized rides, Vada says—in Michigan, Wisconsin, Oklahoma and Florida. They have biked across the country together and also travel together occasionally when not biking, although, as Vada says, "We're kind of letting up." They first met on a bicycle tour of Europe in 1974. They tent together on RAGBRAI. Oh, yes, one more thing: She's 73, he's 68.

From Germany

And here's another, this one from the next day, same year:

Peter and Brigitte Lotz, 42 and 39, respectively, flew from their Elmshorn home in northwestern Germany to Omaha just to ride the Register's Annual Great Bicycle Ride Across Iowa-XX. So what did the Lotzes think of RAGBRAI after six days on the road? "It's great," Peter said. "All the people are so friendly. No one is shouting at anyone. It is just great." The Lotzes flew from Hamburg to London to Chicago to Omaha, then tried three bridges before being directed to Bellevue, Neb., where they were able to cycle across the Missouri. Once on RAGBRAI, they were adopted by the Rainbow Cyclists of Cedar Falls-Waterloo. Will the Lotzes come back? "Yes, of course," Peter said. But here's the best part. After RAGBRAI ends today, the Lotzes have two weeks before they have to return to Germany. They're going to rent a car in Keokuk and—guess what?—spend the two weeks touring the rest of Iowa.

Bob Breedlove

No RAGBRAI book would be complete without a mention of Bob Breedlove. He is an orthopedic surgeon by profession but a bicycle rider by compulsion.

I was talking to him and checking the facts for this piece when he told me that he had not even been a cyclist until he did his first RAGBRAI in 1983, and I muttered something like, "Another burden I have to bear." I'll give you his response to that comment later.

Let me begin by saying that Breedlove is the most compulsive cyclist I've ever met. There are more compulsive cyclists than he out there, but they all ride on the Tour de France, and I've never met them.

What you or I or any other normal person would consider a very difficult bike ride is no more than a warmup for Breedlove. He is an ultra-marathon cyclist.

There is a competition called the Race Across America, or RAM for short. The idea is a bunch of people who have qualified by competing in ultra-marathon rides in their regions of the country get together on bicycles in late summer somewhere on the West Coast and ride like hell to the East Coast. The one getting there first wins. There are categories: Men, women and tandems. Just the same, the concept strikes me, and always has struck me, as insane.

Breedlove has ridden RAM five times.

He has won RAM twice on a tandem, once with equally nutty cyclist Lon Haldeman in 1992 and once with equally nutty cyclist Roger Charleville in 1990. His best finish on a single bike was second place in 1994 in eight days and 15 hours. That's across the entire U.S. of A. on a bicycle in eight days and 15 hours. One has to wonder about the winner.

But wait, that's only the beginning.

Breedlove also has ridden the European race from Paris to Brest, in northwest France, and back—a distance of 700-plus miles—three times, all three on tandems. He has won twice, with Haldeman in 1987 and with Rich Fedrigon in 1991. The third time, Fedrigon took sick. They finished, but well out of the competition.

All of which brings us to Breedlove and RAGBRAI.

As noted above he rode his first one in 1983. "I didn't even own a bike," he told me not too long ago. He borrowed a bike

147

from his younger brother, Dan, of Kewanee, Ill., "and did my first RAGBRAI because everybody else in Iowa was doing it and it seemed like the thing to do."

So that started it. Then he did RAGBRAI again in 1984. "Yeah," he said. "I camped out like everybody else." But then he got serious and got into long-distance racing. RAM and stuff like that.

Then, for the first time in 1990, he decided to do RAGBRAI again, but with a difference. Instead of starting on Sunday morning, like everyone else, he would start on Friday morning at 5 a.m. in the starting town, then ride all day and all night and try to finish in the ending town in 24 hours.

Yes, that's what he did. Year after year after year. Then, in 1996, he decided to rejoin the rest of the world and do RAG-BRAI like a normal human being until Thursday evening. That is, he started on Sunday morning and rode along with the rest of us until the end of the route on Thursday, then he got into a van, drove back to the starting town and set out yet again on Friday at 5 a.m. to do the whole route in 24 hours. "That's the goal, yes," he said, "but it usually winds up about 28 hours because I join up with the ride at some time Saturday and I finish with friends at their pace."

I didn't realize until I talked to him about this piece that he considered the RAGBRAI cycling marathon as his final warmup before RAM. The event used to start about a week after RAG-BRAI ended. This year, however, it is going to start on the Wednesday of RAGBRAI week.

Breedlove was going to compete in RAM again this year, but his son, Bill, 13, wanted to go on RAGBRAI, "and I wasn't going to send him out alone." So Bob is giving up the agony of RAM to attend RAGBRAI with his son. Hey, the guy's a Promise Keeper without telling anyone. What a guy.

This will be Bill's third full RAGBRAI. The Breedloves' three daughters—(ages as of March of 1998) Molly, 20; Ann, 18, and

Erika, 14—all have been on at least parts of RAGBRAI, and Erika was thinking she would go again in the summer of 1998.

Oh, yes, I promised to tell you the final word about Breedlove and bicycling and my role.

"What a life-change that has been for me on a bicycle," he said. "Yeah, I suspect you should take the blame."

And I do.

With pride.

Lorraine Roth

(I have never met Lorraine Roth of Bettendorf, but in 1988 she sent me the following letter, the funniest I've ever received concerning RAGBRAI. The subject is how she trains for the bike ride. I've quoted it with pleasure several times.)

Rather than working on physical exertion I concentrate for two weeks on developing survival skills, including nutritional and schedule variations.

Ingesting a daily pint of Crisco, alternating liquid and solid forms, prepares my digestive system for the endless porkburgers and hamburgers that are to come. An additional half-dozen cookies and two or three quarts each of iced tea, lemonade and water are also minimum daily requirements.

In anticipation of the week's rituals, my daily routines also are altered.

My alarm rings at 3:30 a.m. I push "Play" on my tape deck, and "Campground Sounds I" begins. The familiar sounds of clanking tent stakes, alarm clocks at five-minute intervals and cries of "Come on, Jody, we're burning daylight!" fill the air. A teenager screams as a tent is let down on top of her, followed by loud laughter.

Arising at 5 a.m., I get dressed, make my bed, then stand outside my bathroom door for 37 minutes before entering. I repeat this procedure several times a day. Then, at 4:35 p.m., after my 37-minute wait, I take a breath-takingly icy shower, taking care that the water is cold enough to require a full 10 minutes to rinse out shampoo, with teeth clenched, breath held.

In the evenings, I sit or lie on the floor, and stand by the telephone for 45 minutes before making a call. At the end of the day, I climb into my sleeping bag on the hardwood floor, first having made sure the marbles are strategically placed. I play Side 2 of "Campground Sounds"—similar to Side 1, but with the addition of foul language as bikers trip over tent ropes.

At the end of this strict diet and rigorous training, I am truly prepared for the ride.

Etc.

There are hundreds—no, thousands—more RAGBRAI personalities, you know, if only I could remember their names.

RAGBRAI somewhere in western Iowa, 1986
Ann Karras photo

Carter LeBeau and hands, 1973
Carl Voss photo

155

(Top) *Army surplus parachutes over Kanawha, 1987.* (Bottom) *Cyclists clog streets of Mitchellville, 1988.* Ann Karras photos

157

(Top left) *Dancing in the street at Bremer Station.* (Left insert) *Water bottles for sale, 1990.* (Bottom left) *Dancing in the grass.* (Top right) *Grampa RAGBRAI busses trooper Bill Zenor.* (Bottom right) *Chuck Offenburger addresses the crowd.*

Ann Karras photos

A RECENT EXCAVATION
UNEARTHED THIS FIND WHICH
MAY LINK RAGBRAI TO
EARLIER TREKS. GEOLOGISTS
CONCUR THESE GIANT REPTILES
MIGRATED ANNUALLY IN LARGE
NUMBERS DURING THE MESO
ZOIC PERIOD (180 MILL.B.C.) USING
VARIOUS WHEELED APPARATUS
AS PRIMARY TRANSPORTATION

(Top left) *Members of Team Holstein of Wisconsin, 1990.* (Left insert) *John Karras with a big smile, 1989.* (Bottom left) *A cycling dinosaur in the town of Andrew.* (Above) *The Whistlers of Odebolt, 1988.* Ann Karras photos

(Above top) *Mr. Pork Chop, Paul Bernhard, sold his famous pork chops for $5 apiece in Estherville, 1996.* Photo by Crista Jeremiason, Copyright 1996, The Des Moines Register and Tribune Company. Reprinted with permission. (Bottom left) *Pork chops on the barbecue grill, 1990.* (Bottom right) *Former Des Moines Mayor John (Pat) Dorrian and wife Carolyn.* Ann Karras photos

161

(Above) *An innovative watering contraption.* (Left) *Algona's record long cake and decorator, 1990.*

Ann Karras photos

163

(Top left) *Tent sculpture in Cedar Falls, 1989.* (Left insert) *Taking it easy after a long day, 1988.* (Bottom left) *Cooling off in West Point, 1988.* (Above top) *Important stop on a foggy morning.* (Above bottom) *Relaxing at Crystal Lake.* Ann Karras photos

(Top) *Negotiating Burlington's Snake Alley.*
(Bottom) *Watching the bikers near Cedar Falls,
1989.* (Right) *Climbing the dreaded Pilot Mound
Hill, 1989.* Ann Karras photos

166

(Right) *The drenching
first time in Bellevue,
1989.* (Below) *Dipping
wheels in Bellevue,
1989.* Ann Karras photos

What It All Has Meant There are

those who will tell you that RAGBRAI is nothing but a

week-long drunken orgy of sex and drugs. Not only are

there those who will tell you this, there also are others

who will believe them.

Yes, we have drunks, a wild-party group in our ranks—women who enter wet-T-shirt contests or take their tops off, guys who beer slide naked, people who moon. Many of these people are adults, some from small towns—people of substance where they live—who act like fools on RAGBRAI because they don't dare to act that way at home. RAGBRAI gives them release, an excuse to let go and be outrageous, to relive or perhaps create the teen years they missed.

But I must add that I think RAGBRAI's reputation as a wild party is grossly exaggerated, given much more credence than it actually has. I attribute this partly to a tendency of many people to believe the worst of what they hear despite the obvious evidence of their senses, and partly to another tendency of many people to dwell on the naughty.

The truth of the matter, I stoutly believe, is that the orgy crowd constitutes a relatively small number of the masses that attend RAGBRAI (somewhere between 8,000 and 20,000, depending on the day and area of the state), and tends to congregate at the rear end of the pack.

I say this because I ride somewhere in the middle of each day's pack—never at the front, and only once at the end—and in

(From left) *Donal Kaul, Chuck Offenburger, John Karras and Don Benson, 1992.* Ann Karras photo

all of my years of RAGBRAIing, I have yet to see a bare breast or a naked beer slide.

Oh, the nudes, the public fornicators, the orgiasts are there, all right (just as they are in your home town), but they don't come anywhere near to defining RAGBRAI (or your home town either, for that matter). RAGBRAI is a whole lot more than that, and all of the rest of it is just plain downright wholesome—people helping people, people returning wallets, people letting people into their homes and forming lasting friendships, people enjoying Iowa, people being just plain good people.

RAGBRAI, in these first 25 years, has meant a lot of things to a lot of people—to me, to my wife Ann, to Don Benson, to Jim Green, to Don Kaul, to Chuck Offenburger, to the state of Iowa, to the hundreds of small towns it has passed through, to the thousands and thousands of people from all over the United

States and from around the world who have participated in it, and to the thousands of Iowans who have left their own areas and been introduced to the rest of their state.

RAGBRAI shows Iowa at its very best, and the way it can be seen best—from the seat of a bicycle.

By the end of RAGBRAI-XXV in 1997, more than 165,150 cyclists had pedaled more than 11,500 miles and visited at least 686 Iowa communities.

That, I submit, is impact.

What else has it done for Iowa?

Year after year, it has brought communities together as never before. Many churches and community organizations never pulled together until they faced the challenge of preparing for RAGBRAI. Organizations that had never before cooperated— Knights of Columbus and Masons, for example—got together and found they enjoyed working with each other.

The ride gave communities—and especially the small towns— the chance to showcase their strengths, the most important being hospitality and friendliness, to people from all over the United States and all over the world.

And of course, the influx of money did no harm. Not that every food and lemonade stand and church saw a profit. Occasionally there were disasters, often because the organization did not follow guidelines suggested by *The Register*, but sometimes for no apparent reason. During the early years of the ride communities sometimes had to be persuaded to host RAGBRAI because people equated bikers with motorcycle gangs instead of bicyclists. Now a community never turns down the opportunity without a compelling reason.

Finally, RAGBRAI has proven to thousands upon thousands of cyclists that Iowa, indeed, is not flat, and an equal number no longer confuse Iowa with Idaho or Ohio.

What about those of us who've been intimately associated with RAGBRAI for years? What has it meant to us? Here, in our own words, are the answers.

Don Benson

My best memories were not necessarily of the rides. The best memories were working with the towns, getting ready for the rides. I met so many neat people while laying out the route and making the route changes as necessary. You know the ride itself is, from my point of view and probably from Jim's, too, the ride itself is a big hassle. And my attitude with the ride always was I wanted the riders to see as little of the organization as they possibly could. I wanted the riders to have fun. And I wanted to keep it as unstructured as I could.

So I tried not to get uptight during the ride week. If I was going to get uptight it was going to be beforehand. It was just like when somebody would come up to me and say, and usually a mother, and say my 15-year-old son isn't in yet. We can't find him.

We always took them seriously, but we knew good and well it wasn't anything to get overly excited about because, most likely, the boy was already in and it was the mother who was lost. And this happened just time after time.

Also, anything that had just gone by, as far as I was concerned it was not something to worry about. I didn't worry about anything that had happened. If I was going to worry it was about something that was going to happen, because there wasn't anything I could do about something that had already happened. That was basically my philosophy.

As far as the ride goes, there were some real fun things. ... I can't think of any one thing that stood out more than anything else. I can think of some very pleasant times. Bellevue has always been one of my favorite towns. But the towns aren't anything. They're just buildings. It's the people in the towns, and usually the local committee that I worked with.

There's no better place to do something like that than in Iowa. We've been in every state except North Dakota, we've been in most states two or three times. Iowa fits together in every way. The road system, the fact that there's not a whole lot of difference between the people from one end of the state to the other, the fact that the people are friendly, almost overly friendly sometimes, but they're sincerely friendly, and that's great. There's no place better to have it than here. It's almost like the Netherlands of the United States. It's a bicycle-friendly place.

Chuck Offenburger

I say that RAGBRAI has really changed my whole life. At the time I got involved in 1983, I was not a bicyclist, I was a jogger, but not in very good shape, still smoking and drinking and content with my life. I became a part of RAGBRAI with a little bit of intimidation, jumping into something that had been going on for so long, and I didn't know how I'd fit and get along with everybody.

I'm happy to report 15 years later that it's been an almost unanimously positive change in my life. I've come from not being a bicyclist to being a very dedicated one that not only does RAGBRAI but does rides all over Iowa the rest of the year. Also, RAGBRAI inspired me to ride across the nation in 1995 with 300 other people on our Iowa 150 Bicycle Ride, a Sesquicentennial Expedition.

Subsequent to that I've learned the fun of being on far-ranging bicycle tours, so my wife, Carla, and I are planning now every year to go on another bike tour in another state somewhere around the U.S. In 1996 we did Bike Virginia, in 1997 we did GOBA, which is the Great Ohio Bicycle Adventure.

This year we're planning to ride our bikes along the same route we used in 1995 on the cross-country ride from Muscatine to Centerville, Tenn., to see our good friends the Bateses in June and then we're very likely going to do another ride, probably in Michigan in August, in addition to RAGBRAI.

We're really becoming more and more involved in it all the time. We've now gotten to where we like to ride self-contained and camp out even. I never dreamed I would get to that point, but I do enjoy it.

My health and physical condition are so much better now than when I started. I quit smoking in about 1986, and stayed off of cigarettes until '90, and then when I went and covered the Persian Gulf war I lapsed back into smoking for a year and finally got off of them again in '91.

I don't think I would have ever been able to quit smoking without a lot more effort except for the fact that it was becoming more of an embarrassment to me on RAGBRAI all the time and made getting up the hills too hard because I never had any wind.

When I first started riding—Jim Green and I laugh about it—when we first started riding RAGBRAI together the only way we could get up those big hills was the thought that we'd be able to get off our bikes at the top and smoke a cigarette. I quit drinking in 1989, thank goodness. I live more healthily than I did, I'm much happier than I was.

So I plan to keep doing it. I've become so sold on this that I say every year at the end of RAGBRAI that we're going to keep doing this thing until absolutely everyone in Iowa has done it at least once.

Jim Green

For me it has been an opportunity to work with and be associated with some of the greatest people in the state of Iowa, and to help in the growth process for each one of their communities to be the best that they can be.

The thing that I miss most with this job is that on Sunday morning when RAGBRAI begins and everyone leaves, I can't be on my bike with them. I know from my experience of riding eight of them what that feeling is and I miss it. I'm looking forward to the time I can ride it with my grandchildren on a tandem.

Judy [his wife] has always worked with me. When I started riding in 1983, she was in the information center with Jackie Benson. She is now the key to the campgrounds running smoothly. Our daughter, Joanie, who lives in Alton, organized the town both times we went through there in recent years. It made me feel proud, because her theory is that everyone in the community has to get into it to make it work, and she got that done.

As a parent, when she called me last January and told me that she and her husband, Tag, were going to do RAGBRAI I just laughed. But they trained hard, lost 50 pounds each and did it, and will do it again.

The greatest thing about my job is all the people I get to work with. That is just beyond belief. You, John, and Chuck. I'd put our teamwork up against anyone. We disagree, but we listen to each other, we work to put out the safest route of all for RAGBRAI.

It's wonderful.

Donald Kaul

(I recently asked Kaul to tell me what the ride had meant to him. This was his response.)

I honestly don't know what RAGBRAI means to me. I look upon it as an exercise in Unintended Consequences. It seems to me that the qualities that made it so attractive in the first place attracted so many people that it lost those qualities. On the other hand, I remember the thrill of standing among those 30,000 people on Court Avenue in 1992.

(However, years ago, he wrote the following about RAG-BRAI.)

There is a more positive side to the ride, there's a sense of community about it, a shared experience, which is rare in contemporary life. There is a reality to it. You're not watching other people do something. You're doing something yourself. In a society that seems to be suffocating in vicarious experience, even pain can be a virtue.

Ann Karras

The bike ride changed my life by offering me an opportunity to do what I had always done and liked to do; an outdoor activity. It just happened that biking came along.

When I learned to ride a bike as a child it gave me a freedom I had never known. Traffic was not a major problem and my mother allowed me to ride all over the town (a suburb) of New York City. My bike was transportation to everywhere.

After marriage and children the bike fell into disuse, until my husband became intrigued by ten-speed bicycles. He insisted I get a new bike and so in my early forties I started out again on a bike. Our first major trip was twelve miles long, with our youngest on the back of John's bike and the other three children riding their own.

We all practically had to go to bed the next day. The older three children loved their bikes as I had loved mine, but as many children do they would lose bikes or have them stolen because they forgot they had ridden them somewhere and left them out. After one such incident I yelled so much that John said, "Which is more important, the bike or the child?" I answered, "Obviously, the bike."

The first time I rode 50 miles and survived I got the idea that I might be able to do a really long ride. And then along came a century ride, TOMRV. There was a 50-mile cutoff I had planned to take but no such cutoff appeared and by the end of the day I was still riding. I finished the ride.

In 1973, the year of the first bike ride across Iowa, as with so many women, my husband said I couldn't possibly make that distance. I said that I could. The woman I worked for offered me the week off to do the ride. Now I had the time and the challenge and off I went with Donald Kaul and John on my 10-speed Raleigh Competition in tennis shoes with no helmet and no bike shorts.

Our children wished us well and were quite happy with a sitter even though all but one was a teenager by then.

I went on the first bike ride across Iowa for exactly the same reasons that others, mostly women, have expressed over and over.

"My husband (or someone) said I couldn't do it."

"It gave me some freedom and change from routine."

"It looked like fun."

"I could eat all I wanted and not put on weight." (Not exactly true).

The first bike ride was fun, hard and freedom from everyday routine. Overnight I gained some recognition, got invited out to dinner, ran errands for Don and John because they were swamped with problems. I interviewed Clarence Pickard with only the vaguest idea of how to interview someone. I found out that Iowa was pretty big, pretty hot, and full of friendly people.

The evenings were magical. We spent the summer evenings sitting under lamplight and talking while Bill's Cyclery group repaired bikes. The day's rides did not seem that long because so many people were riding, all of about 250, mostly men. I

175

was sometimes recognized and sometimes called Mrs. Kaul (did you come all the way from Washington?), met so many people and knew everybody on the ride by the end. It was a wonderful year.

There was also a downside to going on the ride. Some give me no credit for doing it. They assume that women stay home and "keep the home fires burning." Even today some people ask me if I have been on the ride and are surprised when I tell them, "all but number VI."

Being pleasant and upbeat all the time because you are on display also can be very tiresome. Only once or twice was I asked to say a few words and that wasn't too difficult.

As I have gotten older the hills have gotten steeper and the miles longer. I used to be one of the fastest riders and now even little kids on three speed bikes pass me going up hills.

I still enjoy biking and I still ride RAGBRAI. It has helped to keep me in shape, made me a role model for some younger women, and given me the false assurance that I could do any sport at any age. I still never think that age is a factor if I really want to try something. And I think success in biking has done this for me.

Our children have not followed in our footsteps because of lack of time. Someday they hope to ride in RAGBRAI.

The ride has created in me a real understanding of the people here. Part of me just loves Iowa but during the heat of summer days I wonder what I'm doing here.

Mara Krumins Neal

(Neal, of Des Moines, wrote a letter to the editor in the fall of 1997 used as "Further Reflections" on *The Register*'s editorial page under the headline, "A Gentle Push on RAGBRAI." In my opinion, it sums up beautifully the feelings that many people have about the bike ride. Ann and I both knew her father, Atis.)

Watching Iowa Public Television's "Living in Iowa" RAG-BRAI special one recent weekend brought tears to my eyes, especially the flashback clips of RAGBRAI-IV. That year was my second ride, the first year that I would ride the whole way.

Over the following years, RAGBRAI would evolve as our family vacation. What started with my father and brother would expand to include my mother, sister, myself and a rainbow of friends. My mother and sister would alternate driving our station wagon, and each night we would set up our huge canvas cabin tent, the RAGBRAI Hilton.

As we children grew up, other things took precedence to a vacation riding a bike. My last ride with my dad was RAG-BRAI-IX. Beginning with X, Dad would go on RAGBRAI with a group of friends who called themselves "The Owls and the Eagles." You know the saying—"He who hoots at night with the owls cannot soar in the morning with the eagles." My dad was always known as an eagle.

In June 1988, my father had surgery to remove cancer from his colon. Six weeks later, he rode one day of RAG-BRAI-XVI. Two weeks after that, we celebrated my wedding to my husband, Gary.

By the end of 1988, my father found the surgery had not been enough. The cancer had spread.

My father died March 28, 1989.

Late summer that same year, my brother gave his Raleigh Super Course to my husband. Originally my dad's, it was handed down to my brother, and finally to Gary. We rode together a few times that fall, and at some point Gary agreed to ride on one RAGBRAI, just to see what my family was talking about.

Which brings us back to the 25th anniversary ride in 1997. It was my 15th ride, the eighth together with my husband.

The 25th ride reminded me of all the gifts my father gave to me. This was brought home to my heart on the first day of

177

the ride this year, 82 miles from Missouri Valley to Red Oak.

Still several miles out of Red Oak, I was riding slowly up another hill. Gary, having more strength on hills, had ridden ahead. Nearing the top, I looked ahead to see a bike turn around and come back down the hill. The man turned again to come up beside his young daughter. She was clearly discouraged and tired by the day's ride. He placed his hand on the small of her back, and gave the push she needed to reach the top.

When I saw him reach over to his daughter, I broke into tears. That little girl could have been me. On those first few RAGBRAIs, when I was 9, 10, 11 years old, my father would come alongside me, and give me the boost I needed.

At the end of the week, standing next to the Mississippi, I cried again. I realized my dad had always been alongside me, to give me guidance when I needed it. I realized it that first day. The rest of the week was saying good-bye, eight years after his death.

Now, in December, I'm looking forward to February, when the next route is announced. Looking forward to seeing the same old friends and meeting new ones. Looking forward to celebrating life in Iowa.

I grew up with RAGBRAI; I hope to grow old with RAG-BRAI.

And I know my dad is always with me, giving me a gentle push.

John Karras

No question, it changed my life, and all for the better.

Because of it, I stopped smoking, kept biking, discovered the beauties of the state of Iowa, met thousands of friendly, decent and upstanding people and a few scoundrels, and formed dozens of friendships that have lasted years and years.

If it hadn't been for RAGBRAI and the discipline of fitness

it imposed on me, I feel certain I would have died of the heart attack I endured in 1987.

But such considerations are mundane. The actuality has been much more romantic. Memories, memories. Many of them glorious, some painful, some hilarious, some stunningly beautiful.

Try to tell someone who's seen Iowa by auto that the state is beautiful and you'll likely be met by a blank stare followed by an expression of incredulity. Put that same person on a bicycle and lead him around the state and he'll understand exactly what you've been saying.

179

I'll never forget that enchanting morning out of Hawarden in 1985, for example, with cyclists silhouetted on the road against valleys full of mist. It was magical. Or my first introduction to the hills of northeastern Iowa, a few of them three miles long, and the thrilling vistas that open up on all sides as the land falls away from the ridge lines into winding, wooded valleys.

There have been other rewards, not the least of which was discovering the yawning emptiness of celebrity. I can say without the smallest pinch of egotism that I became famous in Iowa at the age of 43. I had labored anonymously at *The Register* on the night copydesk, where no one but your colleagues knows your name, for 14 years, and suddenly, because of RAGBRAI and the weekly column I wrote, became something of an Iowa household name.

It was a strange experience. People who didn't know me or anything about me except what they thought they knew from reading my stuff were telling me how much they admired me. This could be heady stuff, if one took it seriously. Also very dangerous. One very easily could begin to believe it.

Actually, I found such attention by virtual strangers to be embarrassing. They didn't really know me. They weren't familiar with my many shortcomings. I was always much more comfortable with the friends who knew me well.

What I have enjoyed most on RAGBRAI, however, and especially in the earlier years, is seeing middle-aged women find independence.

Modern feminism was in its adolescence when RAGBRAI began in 1973, and a lot of women in their 30s, 40s and 50s were still laboring under the illusion that they couldn't do much of anything or go much of anywhere without a man at their side. RAGBRAI helped demonstrate to at least one and perhaps two generations of women that they could pretty much go any damn where they pleased without a guy hanging around. The demonstration dismayed as many traditional men as it pleased traditional women. I was more than pleased to have been a part of its happening.

What else is there to say?

There was a time I thought I could walk away from RAGBRAI without looking back. It was a job, part of my job, I thought, and no more. Then the heart attack struck a week before RAGBRAI-XV. I sat in my front yard on a lawn chair and watched my friends leave, and wanted to yell to them to come back, you can't have a RAGBRAI without me. I realized then, what the ride had come to mean to me.

I wrote a special sendoff piece for the ride that appeared in *The Register* the Sunday morning the ride began:

There's no doubt that a lot of you have felt some shock that someone who has worked as hard as I have to stay in good condition should fall victim to a heart attack. As Walt Gary, a friend from Fairfield who is RAGBRAI's medical director every year, put it on the phone the other night, "What the heck are they going to tell you to do now—get more exercise?"

Well, I haven't been told yet, but I think the message is going to be closer to how I have to change some habits, such as eating a 12-ounce sack of potato chips at a sitting. But enough of that. The fact is that my compulsive exercising very likely saved my life. And at least we don't have to call this the "John Karras Memorial Bike Ride," which is a good thought.

Finally, let me say your expressions of concern in the form of cards, flowers and notes, have, I think, come very close to healing my heart.

RAGBRAI certainly has not been all of my life, but it's been a very large part of it.

It's been a marvelous gift, conceived in innocence, achieved through happenstance and continuing in the unlikeliest of magical manners.

Index

187